GROW YOUR OWN
HERBS IN POTS

GROW YOUR OWN
HERBS IN POTS

35 SIMPLE PROJECTS FOR CREATING BEAUTIFUL CONTAINER HERB GARDENS

deborah schneebeli-morrell

CICO BOOKS
LONDON NEW YORK

To Florez Schneebeli
A ray of sunshine who appeared the day after this book was finished

Published in 2010 by CICO Books
an imprint of Ryland Peters & Small
519 Broadway, 5th Floor,
New York NY 10012

www.cicobooks.com

10 9 8 7 6 5 4 3 2

A CIP catalog record for this book is available from the Library of Congress.

ISBN 978-1-907030-21-5

Printed in China

Project Editor: **Gillian Haslam**
Text Editor: **Eleanor Van Zandt**
Designer: **Elizabeth Healey**
Photographers: **Heini Schneebeli** and **Caroline Hughes**

Contents

Introduction

Herbs can be defined as essentially useful plants: plants in which one or more parts—leaves, flowers, stems, roots, and/or seeds—can be used in some form or for some purpose. Among their numerous uses are as ingredients in cooking, as remedies for disease or common ailments, as insect repellents, as essential oils, and as ingredients in perfume.

Knowledge of the uses of herbs goes back to ancient times. We have been able to study Greek texts dating as far back as the first century A.D. that list herbs and describe their uses. Before the development of modern medicine, herbs played a major role in the treatment of disease, and so these manuscripts, called herbals—which can be found in many museums and libraries—can teach us a great deal about the history and development of medicine, as well as social history. Herbals have been important documents in many cultures. The earliest ones emphasized the role of herbs in myth, magic, and medicine; later ones began to document culinary uses; and the more recent herbals have served as manuals not only on how to use herbs but, more interestingly, on how to grow them.

This is, of course, the beginning of gardening: the growing of plants that are not just for sustenance. You can see how far this has developed, as we now grow an extensive range of plants: those that are purely decorative and others,

Left An old enamel saucepan now provides a home for basil and chili plants.

Right This terracotta bowl made in Crete makes an ideal planter for a useful quantity of flat-leaved parsley.

Far right Thai basil has pretty pink flowers that emerge from dense purple bracts.

such as herbs, that combine beauty with utility. The more we know as gardeners, the more we will be interested in the origins and uses of plants that we grow in our contemporary gardens. We may love a plant for its beauty or its scent, but we are interested in it for its history, its associations, and its uses.

For example, I grow thyme, tansy, and dyer's chamomile in my garden; they are lovely plants, but I find them all the more interesting because I know that thyme oil was used by the ancient Egyptians to embalm mummies, that tansy was once a strewing herb (laid on the floor to deter domestic pests) and was also used to curdle milk, and that dyer's chamomile was used to make the yellow pigment in Turkish carpets. All plants have stories, and herbs have more than most.

Alongside this story of herbs and their uses for mankind are the symbolic, ritual, religious, poetical, and literary references to them. This is a rich field;

you will find mention of herbs in the Bible, in Shakespeare, in poetry—both sentimental and profound—and in folk songs. Surely we all now know the words of "Scarborough Fair," that popular sixteenth-century ballad made so famous by Simon and Garfunkel: "Parsley, sage, rosemary and thyme."

I love this quotation from Sir Thomas More (1478–1535), in which he speaks of the symbolic meaning of the common herb rosemary:

"As for rosemary, I let it run all over my garden walls, not only because my bees love it but because it is the herb sacred to remembrance and to friendship, whence a sprig of it hath a dumb language."

As a bee keeper myself, I am well aware of the plants that bees "love," and throughout this book I mention the many herbs that attract them. It is so important to provide pollen- and nectar-rich plants for pollinating insects, because these little creatures are an important part of the biodiversity of our stressed planet. We ignore their needs at our peril.

Left A mulch of shells below marjoram and oregano plants helps to conserve moisture in the soil as well as reflecting warmth underneath the plants.

Right These tiny orange-and-black grubs are the caterpillars of ladybugs. They are very welcome visitors, as they consume a great many aphids.

Even though many people may know something of this ancient tradition of growing herbs, and about their domestic, medicinal or cosmetic properties, we are often unaware that many of the products we buy are based on herbs that we could grow ourselves. For example, we may buy and use calendula cream from a pharmacist without knowing that it is made with the common pot marigold, one of the easiest plants to grow. Today's reviving interest in herbs should make it possible for us to reestablish our connection with ancient remedies and medicine and perhaps retrieve some of the most effective recipes in the herbalist's repertoire.

Above A healthy crop of curly-leaved parsley, originally bought from the supermarket and now growing in a wooden wine box.

CHAPTER ONE

Getting started

Growing herbs is fashionable, but that is not a good enough reason to grow them! Just plant what you like to eat, and grow some more unusual herbs as an experiment—there are some wonderful culinary treats waiting to be discovered.

The family of plants called herbs is extensive and diverse. We grow them not just for their beauty or their scent but, most of all, for everyday use in the kitchen. As your knowledge and experience grow, along with your culinary skill, you will want to extend the range of herbs that you cultivate. There are many excellent, more specialized, books and magazines available on the subject, and a good herb nursery usually has a web site, with each herb illustrated and described. Gardeners are generous people: not only will they freely share their advice and experience; they will also give you seeds, cuttings, and young plants that are surplus to their needs.

Left Large polystyrene boxes, originally used for transporting fish, now provide stylish containers for growing dill, fennel, caraway, and cilantro.

Below The scent of the garden pink is exquisite. It's a wonderful plant, which will flower all summer.

Bottom This freshly cut bunch of mixed salad and herb leaves contains an interesting array of flavors.

Opposite Cut your herby salad leaves as required, using a large pair of scissors.

Growing herbs

Growing herbs, like growing vegetables, is purposeful gardening. There is nothing complicated about their cultivation—remember that it is natural for plants to grow! You need only provide the right conditions and care in order to make your plants as healthy and productive as they can be. Even a so-called non-gardener can have a pot or two by the back door for growing parsley, mint, thyme, or other popular herbs. If you start with a few pots of herbs, you will soon become engaged with the whole process of growing.

It is quite likely that you will want to grow some vegetables alongside your herbs (even if it is only a few salad varieties in a window box). Both can be grown in containers, some even in the same pot. For example, I always grow basil plants at the base of my pot-grown tomatoes. They go together well in the kitchen, and basil's strong scent is said to deter pests that might affect the tomato plant. To garden organically (and I strongly recommend this method), you should never grow only one group of plants.

Biodiversity is the key; as a gardener you will be providing food and habitats for a number of creatures. Even if you are growing only a few pots of herbs on a balcony, you need to attract pollinating insects; many plants will set seed only after the flowers have been pollinated.

You won't need much equipment for growing herbs in pots, although a few tools are essential: a small trowel, a dibble for making holes in potting mix for large seeds or small seedlings, a bundle of plant markers, and an indelible pen, for identifying the seeds you have planted. It is wise to wear gardening gloves when mixing soil and manure.

You will need to buy potting mix. To enrich the soil for hungry herbs, it's desirable to add some well-rotted (or dried) cow or horse manure, if possible. Inquire at your garden center for possible suppliers of this. There may be extras, such as fine gravel or sharp sand to make the soil more free-draining, particularly for the woody Mediterranean herbs.

Containers

Choosing containers is an enjoyable part of the project. You may visit secondhand stores, flea markets, and even town recycling depots. You can be original and inventive when you find another use for an unusual container. There are many examples of this in the book: for example, the thymes in a steel wok (see page 38), the basil in reused olive-oil cans (page 44), and the herb salad in an old galvanized washtub (page 56).

Choosing which herbs to grow

To some extent, the herbs that you decide to grow will be determined by those that you like to use, and most of them will be for the kitchen. In my home we use herbs every day in simple dishes, and if we don't have any suitable ones available, the resulting meal seems to be missing something. If you eat food from other cultures—and this is a standard feature of urban life—you may want to grow more exotic herbs, such as Thai basil, cilantro, and lemongrass; luckily, these are all fairly easy to grow.

It is hard for me to choose a single favorite herb—they all have their place; and because of their strong characteristic flavors, they are seldom interchangeable in recipes.

Individual herbs are matched with meat, vegetables, and grains for a number of reasons. Tradition plays a part: rosemary is traditionally used with lamb, mint with peas, and basil with tomatoes, for example. Some flavors naturally complement each other, whereas others clash. Sage is wonderful cooked with potatoes or pumpkin but would taste awful chopped in a salad. Curiously, sage works well with liver; they have a similar element of bitterness

in their flavor. Another consideration is whether the herb helps digestion. For example, rosemary, thyme, and sage seem to be able to help the digestion of fat and so are used with fatty meats. A mixture of crushed fennel seeds (a well-known digestive herb) and coarse sea salt makes an excellent rub for slow-roasted fresh side pork.

The flavor, uses, and characteristics of a number of herbs are described in the projects that follow on pages 38–141.

I would suggest starting off with a few herbs that you know you will use in your cooking, a couple for use in teas, and perhaps one or two that you grow for their scent and beauty. As you learn more about this interesting and extensive subject, you may like to add a few more exotic herbs and to grow others for making simple salves, infusions for baths, or hair rinses; still others could serve as effective repellents for moths and other insects in the home. This is a thoroughly good idea, because most of the proprietary brands that you can buy contain toxic chemicals.

The lists that appear on the following pages may help you choose which herbs to grow, but remember that many of these herbs fall into more than one category: mint, for example, is used in the kitchen and also as a tea.

Left A wooden crate and an old drawer, salvaged from a broken chest, make great containers for basil and mint. Keep pots or containers of everyday herbs close to the kitchen door, so they are always on hand.

Above Blackcurrant sage

Above Violas

Below Borage

Everyday herbs for the kitchen

These are some of my favorite herbs.

**a good basic selection
for beginners**

parsley

chives

sage

rosemary

thyme

mint

basil

marjoram/oregano

**add these if you are a
more adventurous cook**

chervil

garlic chives

fennel

dill

cilantro

Thai basil

lemongrass

sorrel

tarragon

winter and summer savory

**for the pleasure of the intense
fragrance (and flowers)**

pennyroyal

'Treneague' chamomile

blackcurrant sage

pineapple sage

geraniums (pelargoniums)

for herbal teas

fennel

mint

lemon verbena

bee balm (monarda)

lemon balm

chamomile

for edible flowers

nasturtiums

borage

viola

pot marigold

rocket

chives

for garden color and interest

perilla

red-veined sorrel

bronze fennel

red orache

for healing

aloe vera

houseleek

to repel moths

lavender

for the cat!

catnip

Growing characteristics

Herbs can also be classified according to their manner of growth.

Above Chives

annuals

These plants are grown afresh from seed each year. You sow seeds in spring, and the whole cycle of the plant, from germinating to flowering and making seed, takes place over the next few months, finishing by the end of summer.

Examples: basil, coriander (cilantro), nasturtiums

biennials

You sow the seeds one year and the plant makes seed in the summer of the following year.

Examples: parsley, dill

perennials

You can either sow seed or plant young plants; the plant will die back each fall and regrow each spring.

Examples: fennel, lovage, chives, mint

evergreen shrubs

These have a woody structure and grow into long-lasting bushes. They keep their leaves all year and can be clipped into a tidy shape.

Examples: lavender, sage, rosemary, thyme

tender herbs

These are perennials but will survive only if they are brought inside in the winter. Generally they do not like the cold and wet.

Example: lemongrass (aloe vera is also a tender herb but does not die back in the winter).

Below Thai basil

Above Lovage

Left Marjoram

Below Nasturtiums

Growing organically

Thankfully the trend in gardening is very much in the direction of organic practices. This is a relief: we should work with nature, not against it. Gardening organically is not complicated; it has an inherent logic and sense—it is a complete system. You can't just focus on the plants that you want to grow; you must also think about the soil. A healthy, balanced soil will go a long way toward producing healthy, robust plants, which are able to withstand damage from the occasional pest or common disease.

Although it is difficult to be a completely organic gardener, if you are growing your plants in containers, you can try to be as organic as possible. Inevitably, you will need to buy some potting mix to fill your containers, but selecting the right kind for organic gardening is less than straightforward. At the moment, there is no national accreditation body for the use of the term "organic" on bags of potting mix, so you will have to trust the label. More importantly, you should have a compost heap; in fact, you can't really be an organic gardener without one (see page 24). It is simple to build your own, and as well as reducing the garbage sent to landfill, you will produce wonderful free compost that you can add to the bags of commercial mixes that you must buy.

Soil or potting mix does not need added artificial fertilizers, which are used excessively. Although they do boost growth, they do nothing to improve the structure of the soil. In fact, it is highly likely that they will damage a fragile ecosystem, which is so vital to creating the best conditions for your plants. If you do need to increase the fertility of the soil, use some of the organic feeds on the market. Liquid seaweed is rich in nutrients and is a valuable natural fertilizer, used sparingly. Some herbs prefer to grow in a rich soil; where this is needed, I have suggested mixing in a little well-rotted manure (if available).

Please don't use pesticides; these will kill beneficial insects—not just those that you think may be damaging your plants. Some of the major problems that we have with the loss of honeybees and other pollinating insects are caused by extensive and reckless use of pesticides in agriculture and in the garden. They may also damage your own and your children's health.

Most people who want to grow vegetables or herbs at home do so because they want to know where their food has come from and to make sure that it has not been treated with any toxic chemicals. This is very important to many people; we know something about the amount of spraying of commercially grown crops, and if we were fully informed about the extent of this, a lot of us would find it hard to buy food that is not organic.

Above Marjoram flowers are very attractive to butterflies. They reach deep into the flower to seek out the sweet nectar.

Left If you have space to grow comfrey, try it because it is a miraculous plant. Its leaves make a rich compost; an infusion makes an excellent liquid feed. Bees love it, too.

Choosing containers

Above This decorative birdcage makes a very pretty planter with a collection of colorful nasturtiums tumbling through the bent wire frame.

If you have an outdoor space—a garden, balcony, or terrace—you may consider it an outdoor room in the summer and want to give it the same attention that you might give to decorating a room inside your house. You will have a table, chairs, perhaps a place to relax or recline. And because the space is outside you will want to grow plants there. A container-grown herb garden fits well with the current interest in extending the house into the garden.

What you choose to grow your herbs in will be important. There are many pots and planters available from garden centers and homeware stores. The range is vast, far exceeding the conventional (but still attractive) terracotta flowerpot. Materials and colors are enormously varied—including stone, metal, plastic, and glazed ceramics; but there really is no need to spend a lot of money on planters for your herbs. Instead, you can make use of a variety of unusual containers—either bought, found, or recycled—adapting these, where necessary, to make practical planters for your herbs and to extend your style of living outside.

If you are growing your herbs on a balcony, weight may be a problem. Conventional pots are heavy, but a brightly colored plastic or rubber tub (see page 120) —a most practical container in the house and

garden—is really light. It also conveniently has two carrying handles. Polystyrene boxes (see page 62), used to transport fish, are light and practical, and large enough to hold a fair amount of potting mix. Even baskets—especially plastic ones, which will not rot—make excellent lightweight planters (see page 134), so long as you line them with a plastic bag to stop all the water from quickly draining away.

If weight is not an issue, large recycled catering pans are ideal (see page 66). I found two, each large enough to contain a mixed herb garden, on a visit to my local recycling center. I love old pans and teapots, especially if they are colored enamel. There is an amusing irony about growing food in pots used to prepare it! Old galvanized washtubs and buckets make brilliant containers. Although these are highly sought after, there are still, fortunately, many to be

found. Try secondhand stores, flea markets, and even fashionable décor shops.

In Europe it is almost a convention to grow some herbs, particularly basil, in attractive recycled olive-oil cans (see page 44). These are far too nice to throw away, so why not collect a number of them, with a variety of printed designs, and grow a collection of different herbs all in a row?

It is important to select the right container for the herb. Some of the larger herbs need a larger, deeper container. Fennel, for example, has deep roots, and these need space in which to grow; a chimneypot (see page 94) makes a perfect planter, as well as being an interesting piece of architectural salvage.

Some of the quicker-growing herbs will grow in shallow potting mix, but avoid really small containers. I have seen plastic milk bottles and small baked bean cans recommended as containers, but I urge you not to bother with such things. You will only be disappointed, and your plants will suffer from unnecessary stress. Remember that the smaller the pot, the quicker the soil will dry out, and you will inevitably lose some plants to drought.

Above left Curly parsley will grow well in deep soil in a wooden box, but it should not be placed in hot sun.

Above center These hardy houseleeks (*Sempervivum*) will grow to form a dense mat of rosettes.

Above An old colander makes a witty and practical planter for low-growing herbs such as nonflowering 'Treneague' chamomile.

Below Apple mint will grow well in this teapot for one season; then plant it in a bed.

Preparing containers

When planting an unusual container, it is important to adapt or convert it so that it will function effectively as a place in which to grow your herbs. Before planting each herb or sowing seeds, you will need to know what conditions the plant prefers. Some plants—especially those grown in larger, solid-walled containers—will need to have broken crocks, gravel, or crushed polystyrene in the base for drainage before the potting mix is added. However, this may not be necessary in smaller containers—especially those that are fairly porous—as the excess moisture will drain away or evaporate quite quickly.

Baskets must always be lined. A potting mix bag is ideal (use it with any writing on the inside), although any tough plastic bag will be fine for lining a smaller basket. Be sure to make a few drainage slits in the base of the bag before inserting it into the basket. For a more open wire basket or a birdcage (see page 130), use a converted hanging basket liner; these can be bought in shaped pieces or as a length that can be cut to fit. They have the advantage of being flexible, natural-looking, and available in natural colors, such as green or brown.

Containers made from the hardest materials—for example, the steel wok (see page 38) or the galvanized washtubs and buckets and even the large metal pans—will need to have drainage holes drilled in the base (see opposite). For thinner or softer metal, you can use a hammer and a thick, long nail to make the holes.

Chimneypots can be beautiful objects, and because they are tall, they will contain a good depth

Above Low-growing thyme plants will eventually form a dense mat of hightly scented herbs in this wok.

Right This large metal basket, lined with a hanging basket liner, makes a good planter for the onion family.

of potting mix. It is best to stand them on soil, so that they can drain into this. If you don't have a garden, stand the pot in a large saucer-shaped container, but you will need to add some gravel at the base of the pot to aid drainage.

Herbs need the best conditions and thoughtful attention. Throughout the projects in this book, you will find advice on the type of soil, the best size of container to match the needs of your plant, and the final growing position—all considerations to give the herbs the best chance of success. If you grow the herbs properly, you will be rewarded with a useful and healthy crop. You will also learn about the needs and habit of your plant and, more importantly, why and how plants grow.

Drilling holes in containers

I found these very large aluminum catering pans (below) at my local recycling center. They seemed perfect—and rather witty—containers in which to plant my most-used kitchen herbs (see page 66). Since they are made of rather thick metal, my usual method of punching drainage holes with a hammer and nail would not work, so I used a drill to make holes in them, as I did in the steel wok featured on page 38.

1 Turn the pot upside down and rest it on a firm surface. Fit a cordless drill with a large bit (gauge N) suitable for drilling through metal. Drill a ring of six equidistant holes in the base, then drill a seventh hole in the center. You will need some strength to push the bit into the metal, although aluminum is not as hard as steel or iron.

2 If you want to site your container on a roof terrace or balcony, where weight may be an issue, broken polystyrene packaging makes excellent lightweight "crocks" to put in the base for drainage. In a large container you will need a layer about ¾ inch deep.

Potting mixes and soil

It is no exaggeration to say that the most important element in gardening is the quality of the soil. If you are growing vegetables in a garden, it will take a number of years to build up the fertility of your soil. The soil needs to be balanced. This means that it has enough essential nutrients and a good structure (achieved by adding compost and leaf mold), which will support the microorganisms that help to create a healthy, productive growing medium for your crops.

Growing in containers presents a problem where soil is concerned. You obviously need all the same elements as you would from an open soil to ensure a healthy crop, but you must buy and/or make the soil yourself. There are many suppliers of potting mix—also called commercial compost—many of whom claim that their product is organic. Availability of good bagged potting mix will depend on which products your local garden center stocks. Luckily, there are organic mixes that can be bought online, and a small investment of time and research will help you to source the right mix for your needs.

The use of peat compost is generally discouraged by most gardeners and horticultural organizations due to the depletion of natural resources. In the past, peat has been a valuable growing medium for the horticultural industry; today new products, such as coir, composted bark, and recycled waste, are proving effective alternatives. Always try to buy peat-free compost so that you are not contributing to the demise of ancient peat bogs—I discourage my British readers from using peat moss, as this resource has become seriously depleted here. However, in North America, where supplies of peat (mainly in Canada) still total some 270 million acres, peat moss remains an important component of most commercial mixes.

Choosing potting mix

For growing plants in containers, you can choose from a huge range of potting mixes, suitable for different plants and their needs. Here in Britain we can buy commercial composts labeled "John Innes No. 1/No. 2/No. 3," which are loam-based recipes containing increasing amounts of nutrients, as required for plants at different stages of growth. You should be able to find comparable loam-based products from a good garden center. Or, if you wish, you could construct your own potting mix, using loam, sand, well-decayed homemade compost (see below), and some damp peat moss.

For plants requiring a lighter soil I have specified a multipurpose potting mix. To this you can add some decomposed leaf mold or well-rotted manure (that is, well aged and fully decomposed cow or horse manure), if available, for hungry plants. For sun-loving Mediterranean herbs, you can, instead, add some sharp sand or gravel to make a looser, free-draining soil.

Making compost

I recommend that you start your own compost heap. Many gardeners are devoted compost makers, and it is not difficult to find advice on the best methods to use. A simple heap with closed sides is good; throw all your kitchen scraps, peelings, etc., onto it (but not

cooked food, meat, or breads, for fear of rats). I add occasional layers of straw or torn paper and cardboard to build up the proportion of carbon in the mix; green waste tends to generate mainly nitrogen. If space is limited, use a closed system; these are large plastic containers with a close-fitting lid. It should take about six months for the compost to be ready. You will know when it is: the compost should be dark, crumbly, and full of small, red worms. It should look like purchased potting mix and not smell.

If you have even less space, invest in a vermicomposting bin. This contains a colony of worms, which will greedily digest all your kitchen waste and produce in return wonderful dark compost and a nutrient-rich liquid that can be drained off from a tap at the base of the wormery.

The compost that you make can be added to general-purpose potting mix and used for planting. However, do not use this for sowing seeds, because it will contain organisms that can cause "damping-off" of your young seedlings. This is a rot that affects the stem and causes the plants to die. Also, weed seeds in homemade compost may germinate and compete with the seeds you have sown. Instead, buy a seed starting mix: a sterilized mixture that will have just the right amount of nutrients and fertilizer to give your seedlings a good start.

Left This young red orache seedling will grow into a tall decorative herb if planted in deep, rich potting mix.

Feeding plants
Container-grown plants need feeding after some weeks to boost fertility. Liquid seaweed is one of the best organic products. Follow the instructions for the dilution of the concentrated liquids and do not overuse them.

Sowing seeds

In the depths of winter, I yearn for the longer days and the coming of spring, when all gardeners, as well as their gardens, experience an intense burst of activity. By comparison winter can seem somewhat inactive, although you will have the compensation of being able to read through seed catalogs, with their enticing descriptions of herbs, vegetables, and flowers that you may want to grow. This is the point at which you may decide to grow some of the more unusual or exotic herbs.

A good catalog can be an interesting read, and some nurseries give an excellent description of the characteristics of each plant. (Most catalogs can also be read online.) A seed catalog from an herb nursery will also describe the flavor and the use of each herb. I love to read these catalogs: it makes me optimistic and full of anticipation for the growing season.

Alternatively, you can peruse the racks of seeds in a good garden center, picking out various packets and reading the back to discover the characteristics of a plant, the growing conditions needed for it, and the sowing and cropping times. Seeds are expensive; however, I find the widely available Italian packets contain more seeds (and are thus better value) and offer a good variety of herbs. Keep your seed packets in an airtight container in a cool, dry place. Some gardeners use the fridge; I put mine in the garden toolshed.

Growing from seed

Seeds want to grow: they are programmed to germinate when sown at the right time and when given the right conditions. Ideally, they need a good sterile seed-starting mix. This is very important. Don't use garden soil or homemade compost, because these will contain bacteria that could potentially damage young seedlings. The seeds also need warmth, light when they germinate, and moisture. Never let your seed trays dry out completely and never overwater. The seeds will thrive in an even temperature.

Early in the year, you can sow seeds in pots or trays and place them on an inside windowsill where you can look after them. You don't have to use special seed trays, modules, pots, or cells, although these are useful if you have them. You can use all sorts of packaging material; plastic trays with hinged lids are great—the kind that supermarkets package bush fruits in; they are a kind of mini-cloche, with the added advantage of drainage holes! Eggboxes,

toilet tissue tubes, yogurt pots are all fine; place them on a tray to hold the water that drains out. Or you could use a small plastic dishwashing bowl: make a few drainage holes in the bottom. Place a piece of glass or plastic over the top of the tray or bowl to form a cloche.

In late spring you could make a larger mini cloche for your seed trays and pots out of a clear plastic storage box—one that has a lid to keep in the warmth. As the seedlings emerge and become stronger, the lid can be moved aside or be propped on sticks to allow the warm daytime air to circulate. Always close the lid at night, and never leave it on when the sun is very hot during the day, or you may scorch the young seedlings with the buildup of heat.

Below Once you have planted your seeds, it's a good idea to tuck the seed packet into the side of the container, to remind you what you have planted where.

Growing basil from seed

You will need

basil seeds: sweet basil and purple basil

two seed trays

seed-starting mix

plant markers and pen

1 Fill the trays with seed-starting mix and firm this down with your hands. Pour some seeds of one of the basils into your hand and, with the other, sprinkle them thinly across the surface of the mix. Sow the other variety in the same way and label each seed tray.

2 Sprinkle the mixture over the surface so that the seeds are lightly covered. Press the mixture down firmly with your hand.

3 Water the trays gently, using a fine rose on the watering can, and place them in a warm place. Keep the surface of the mixture moist, but not wet.

Seeds for sowing later in the year can be sown outside, either in little pots, as described above, or in the containers intended for them; examples include arugula, coriander, sorrel, and fennel.

Caring for seedlings

When the seedlings have two true leaves (not the first leaves, which appear just after germination), they are ready to be "pricked out"—that is, taken from the seed tray and planted into new pots of compost, where they can be spaced more widely (see basil, page 44).

Another technical term, "hardening off," simply means acclimatizing your young plants to outside survival: leaving them out in the day and bringing them in at night until they adapt to the new, cooler temperatures. When the nights are warmer and the young plants sturdier, they are ready to remain outside day and night.

Sowing seeds and waiting for them to germinate is one of the greatest of pleasures. Witnessing the beginning of life fills you with wonder and optimism; and as a gardener you have the extraordinary privilege of following the whole cycle from seed sowing to seed gathering, all in one season.

Below Place your trays of seeds in a clear plastic storage box; this makes a perfect cloche. Keep the lid on at night and slightly askew during the day, to let the air in.

Buying plants

In the projects that follow on pages 38–141, I have stated where I think it is sensible to buy plants and where I think sowing seed is better or more economical. Most herbs can be grown from seed, but many will take some time to reach maturity, so it makes sense to buy these to start off your herb garden and then graduate to sowing seeds if you want to.

The advantage of buying plants from a specialist nursery is that you will have access to many varieties of one type of herb. This applies particularly to the mints and thymes, of which it is worth growing more

than one kind. I grow common thyme but also couldn't be without the marvelous citrus taste of lemon thyme in the kitchen. Equally, I use a different mint for tea (favoring Moroccan mint) from the one I may use in cooking. A good garden center will have a wide selection of young herb plants for sale, but a specialist herb nursery will have an astonishing variety available, as well as good descriptions and advice about how to grow them.

Although browsing through a catalog can be inspiring, there's a lot to be said for actually seeing the herbs growing—perhaps at a plant fair or, of course, at a nursery. For example, you might not be inclined to buy blackcurrant sage from looking at a picture of its rather boring-looking leaves, but if you were to see it in flower as a mature plant, you would certainly not be able to resist buying at least one. I have often gone to a nursery with a list of herbs that I need and then come home with a collection of more unusual herbs that I knew little about. On my last visit to my favorite herb nursery, I returned with licorice and Korean angelica plants, among other discoveries!

When you have been growing herbs for a while and you have friends who love gardening, you find an added source of new plants. Gardeners are happy to give seeds, seedlings, young plants, and cuttings that they have propagated themselves. In some respects this is the best way to acquire plants: you associate them with the generosity and skill of friends and acquaintances. I have plants in my garden that I have acquired in this way. A plant can live on long after the donor has died—life continues and memories are stimulated.

Far left Although Thai basil is easy to grow from seed, you may only need a couple of plants, so it makes sense to buy them.

Left Some herb nurseries sell very young seedlings, such as these basil plants. Keep them inside until the weather warms up.

Below When you see it in flower, it is not difficult to see why this beautiful variety of blackcurrant sage is called 'Hot Lips'!

Taking cuttings

Taking cuttings is a good way of propagating new plants from existing mature plants. As with sowing seed, taking cuttings seems like a magical process: the plant's ability to produce roots on a cut stem or tip never ceases to amaze and enchant. The technique is not difficult, although some herbs will root more readily than others. Be prepared to wait some weeks for results, and resist the temptation to tug at the cutting to see if roots have developed.

Five types of cutting

1 Softwood These are taken early in the year, before the stems and shoots have become hard, or woody. Take the shoots from nonflowering tips, cutting them about 4–5 inches long, using a sharp knife. Remove the lower leaves and plant the cutting in a gritty potting mix. The cuttings will benefit from some warmth. Keep the mix moist; it may help to spray the cuttings with a fine mist of water.

2 Semiripe The shoots are more mature and cuttings are taken in the summer. Treat them in the same way as softwood cuttings; however, they are hardier and will need a more free-draining potting mix. Place the cuttings in a cool greenhouse or outside, out of the sun; keep them moist, but don't overwater.

3 Hardwood Somewhat tougher stems are taken at the end of the season, in the fall. Use the same methods as for softwood and semiripe cuttings,

but use a free-draining potting mix. Be very careful not to overwater. Place the cuttings in a greenhouse or cold frame over the winter. This kind of cutting needs patience: you may not see success until the following year.

4 Root cuttings These are taken either early or later in the year. The method is particularly suitable for herbs with wandering and vigorous roots. Examples: mint, bee balm, and lemon balm.

5 Layering This is a way of encouraging a parent plant to make new roots on a section of stem still attached to the plant. A low, vigorous branch—of thyme, rosemary, or sage, for example—is pinned into a shallow trench in the potting mix, where it is stimulated to produce roots. The rooted stem is severed and replanted to form a new plant.

Taking semiripe cuttings

Here is the process for taking cuttings from sage and rosemary plants.

1 Take your cuttings early in the morning, from nonflowering tips, and keep them moist in a clear plastic bag or in a jar containing a little water or inside a moist washcloth. Fill a pot with loam-based potting mix with added sharp sand for drainage.

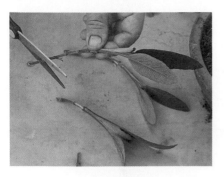

2 Cuttings should be about 5 inches long. Using very sharp scissors or a knife (must be sharp, so as to make a clean cut and not damage the stem), trim the shoot (here sage) just below a leaf joint. This is the area where new roots will emerge.

3 Remove most of the leaves with a sharp knife, and trim the tops from the two remaining leaves at the tip of the cutting. This is done so that the cutting will need less water or strength to protect its leaves; all the energy will go into forming roots.

4 Prepare the rosemary cuttings in the same way, making a neat, clean cut just below a leaf joint. Remove the leaves from the stem, leaving a few at the top.

5 You can trim the tops in the same way as you did with the sage. (This is optional, but I always do it.) The cuttings should measure approximately 4 inches.

6 Use a dibble to make a few holes around the edge of the pot. These need to be deep enough to cover the stem of the cuttings where the leaves have been removed.

7 Push the cuttings into the holes and firm the mixture around them. Push the sage cuttings into the mix in the same way around the edge of the pot.

8 Cover the mixture with some fine gravel; this will reduce the need to water so often. Water the pots with a fine rose and place them outside, but out of direct sunlight. Water occasionally, but never allow the pots to become drenched. Excessive watering is one of the reasons that cuttings may fail.

taking cuttings | **33**

Harvesting herbs

Gather your herbs as you need them. Pick the larger leaves first, from the outside of the plant. Cutting stems and pinching out shoots will encourage plants to grow in a more dense and bushy habit. Pick basil from the top; this prevents it from flowering too quickly and encourages branching out. Other herbs, particularly the shrubby ones, can be clipped and shaped to maintain a tidy shape, but don't cut into the woody growth during the winter months; this risks damaging the plant, and it is less able to recover when it is cold.

My preference is to use fresh herbs all year round, rather than resorting to dried ones. I enjoy the cycle of the seasons, and anyway I don't feel like eating basil in the winter, when there are no fresh home-grown tomatoes to go with it. I like the fallow period

and look forward to the yearly ritual of planting my basil seeds, along with other annual herbs. I love to see the herbaceous herbs send out new shoots in the spring—these always taste the sweetest.

Having to forgo some herbs in cold weather is not really such a hardship. Even though you can't expect to gather fresh basil leaves at Christmas, you could still have rosemary, sage, bay, thyme, marjoram, winter savory, and many others to use on roasts and in winter casseroles. Parsley and chervil will grow happily outside in a mild winter. When the temperature drops, cover them with a frost blanket to protect them from the worst weather.

An exception to my policy of not drying herbs would be those that I grow to make tea, such as peppermint or lemon verbena. Strip the leaves from

Left Although not strictly an herb, these green onions have been picked from a basket containing its close relatives: chives, garlic chives, and leeks.

Right This generous bunch of soft-leaved herbs is ready for use in the kitchen. It consists of basil, chervil, parsley, tarragon, chives, and fennel.

the mint stems and lay them on a dish towel; they will dry quickly in a warm, dry place. Store them in a linen bag if you are going to use them straight away; otherwise store them in an airtight container. Lemon verbena leaves dry very quickly, soon becoming brittle. The fragrance seems even more powerful when the leaves have dried.

I do collect fennel and coriander (cilantro) seed to store for winter use. Pick the whole seed head on a dry day and hang it upside down in a paper bag in a warm, dry place. When the seeds are dry (this may take up to two weeks), store them in an airtight jar. Green (unripe) fennel seed is worth using fresh; its strong aniseed flavor makes a delicious digestive tea.

Flowers and petals should also be gathered on a dry day. Lay them out on a dish towel in a warm, dry place. Bee balm (monarda) petals should be picked off individually from the flower head as they open. It may take a few days to harvest all the delicate petals from one flower head. I dry them outside, although I avoid placing them in direct sunlight, so as to preserve the color better. Store them in an airtight jar. (I sometimes open a jar of dried bee-balm flowers just to breathe in the exquisite summer fragrance.) Chamomile flowers can be dried in bunches hung upside down in a cool, dry place. Remove the flowers from the stems when dry and store in the same way as other herbs.

Gather bunches of fragrant herbs to hang under the hot faucet when you are running a bath. Mint,

lavender, rosemary, and thyme are all perfect for a scented, relaxing soak.

I love the small bundles of fresh mixed herbs that you can buy in French markets – perfect for customers who do not grow their own pot herbs. They dry beautifully, and the flavor is greatly intensified. They make lovely gifts and can be stored for future use.

Below These little bunches of woody Mediterranean herbs are similar to those sold in French markets. They are made up of rosemary, sage, thyme, oregano, golden marjoram, and winter savory.

CHAPTER TWO

Cook's herbs

Adding herbs to a recipe takes your food to another level. There are a number of herbs that every respectable cook should grow; and, in all cases, fresh leaves are superior to dried herbs. Supermarkets have realized this and now sell pots of live herbs, but these are always crammed full of seedlings, which will have a short life. Instead, grow your own herbs at home in pots. The flavor will be stronger and your plants will last longer because you will space them in the pot and use a potting mix that will have enough nutrients to feed the plants throughout the season.

The projects in this chapter will give you ideas and information on how to grow the most commonly used herbs. These are the perennials, such as sage, rosemary, thyme, chives, and mint, as well as those that you need to sow or plant each season, such as my favorite, the clove-scented basil, and parsley, the most useful herb in the kitchen. Some more unusual varieties are also included.

Assorted thymes in a steel wok

Thyme has long been a favorite herb, not only with gardeners but also with cooks, who value its strong flavor. When choosing a young plant, rub your hand over it to release the oil so you can choose the scent that suits you best. If ordering from a catalog, pay close attention to the description, as specialist growers will be able to recommend the best varieties for your conditions.

There are far too many species and varieties of thyme to mention here, but lemon thyme is an especially lovely herb, with many uses in the kitchen. The lemon flavor is quite pronounced; a few sprigs baked with fish or strewn across a tray of onions and pieces of pumpkin, along with some drizzled olive oil and whole crushed garlic cloves, will produce a truly delectable dish. Thyme is often used in a marinade for meat, and a few sprigs infused in olive oil make a lovely cooking oil. It is widely known as one of the main ingredients of "mixed herbs" or, as the French more elegantly describe it, a "bouquet garni." Bees love thyme, which gives their honey a distinctive, powerful flavor; thyme-flavored

you will need

old steel wok or similar, at least 20 inches in diameter

power drill with a bit that can be used on metal (optional)

soil-based multipurpose potting mix

sharp sand or fine gravel

¾ inch gravel

⅜ inch pea gravel

six or so assorted thyme plants, such as lemon thyme, common thyme, variegated thyme, woolly thyme, golden thyme, orange-scented thyme

Opposite This wide, shallow container makes a perfect planter for an assortment of thymes. Cover the bare soil with gravel or pottery shards to absorb the heat of the sun.

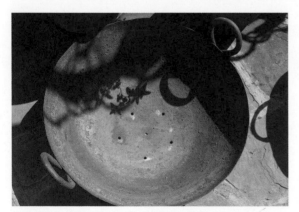

1 Drill six holes in the base of the wok, using a power drill. If you don't feel confident about doing this yourself, a metal workshop or car mechanic can easily do it for you, but it really isn't difficult—it just takes a little longer than drilling through wood.

2 Place a few handfuls of the larger gravel in the wok; this is essential to aid drainage. Thymes hate to be sitting in wet soil.

3 Mix the sand and potting mix together to make a more gritty medium. The amounts are not critical, but I would add at least 1 part sand to 6 parts of potting mix. Add the mixture to the wok, filling the container to within 2 inches of the rim.

4 Soak the potted thymes in a bucket of water for a few minutes, remove from the pot, and tease out the roots before planting. This will encourage the roots to grow outward and into the potting mix, allowing each plant to establish itself more quickly.

5 Make holes in the potting mix 8 inches apart and insert the plants into these holes, pressing the mix around them firmly. Arrange the different thymes according to color and height, placing the lower-growing thymes around the edge of the container.

6 Finally, add the pea gravel, covering the potting mix all around the plants. This helps to retain moisture and makes a surface that will retain and radiate the heat of the sun.

tip
Thyme's natural habit is to spread, so give your young plants space and plant them at least 8 inches apart. Over a short time, they will spread and grow together, making a lovely patchwork.

Opposite Thyme flowers, although tiny, are greedily sought out by bees. The young thyme plants will soon spread out and tumble over the rim of the rusty wok.

honey is widely produced in Greece. From a scientific point of view, thyme has the advantage of breaking down fatty food and will help digestion.

Growing thyme

A hardy, evergreen, low-growing plant, thyme has an undemanding nature. It thrives in poor soil and loves the heat of the sun. I have seen it growing high in the Swiss Alps, where it is collected by locals to make a mild antiseptic tea. It is also mixed with other Alpine herbs to make a much-prized infusion.

To maintain the shape of the plant, trim it after the flowers have faded in late summer. To propagate more plants, take softwood cuttings early in the summer from nonflowering shoots (see page 32).

Alternatively, in late spring detach longer sprigs that have produced small aerial roots along the stem. Pot them up individually in a gritty potting mixture.

Being evergreen, thyme is a versatile herb which can be picked and used throughout the year. A winter picking won't yield quite the intensity of flavor that the summer sun will impart to the herb, but the flavor will still be worth having, and fresh herbs in the winter are a welcome treat.

Thyme oil has powerful antibacterial properties. It is used widely by bee keepers to kill the destructive varroa mite in hives and has been successful in killing mosquito larvae. Even a small amount of the essential oil is toxic and should be used only under professional direction and never ingested.

Choosing your container

It is important to grow thyme (a mixture of several varieties looks lovely) in a wide, low container. I found this large rusted steel wok—evidently from a Chinese restaurant—at my local town dump, destined for recycling. It has now been found a use as the perfect planter for a mixture of low-growing thymes. I drilled holes in the base for drainage and planted a number of thymes in a mixture with added sharp sand (to reduce the fertility and further improve drainage). Make sure to place the planter in full sun. It will serve as an unusual garden decoration, as well as a source of one of the most useful kitchen herbs.

For a decorative planter like this, choose thyme plants with different scents, flavors, and growing habits; also think about leaf color and flower tones. There are some lovely variations with silver, variegated, and golden leaves and a range of flower color from pink, purple, and lilac to white.

Chervil in a fire grate

Chervil is a much underrated herb, which deserves to be more widely grown. I can't recommend it highly enough, especially as it is so easy to grow. Its delicate, low-growing, fernlike leaves have a delicious, subtle flavor, somewhere between parsley and aniseed. The leaves are not that suitable for cooking, so they are nearly always used fresh. At home we often use it liberally in a mixed-leaf salad or tossed with butter over boiled new potatoes. It is a marvelous herb for fish and is brilliant with fava beans, chicken, and egg dishes. I think of it as a French herb, as it is so widely used in French cooking.

Growing chervil

A truly hardy herb, chervil can easily be grown throughout the winter (a fresh herb in the winter is a rare and desirable ingredient). In fact, chervil sown in high summer may run to seed, producing a weak plant that has had its flavor compromised. Chervil is attractive to slugs, so be vigilant, especially when the seedlings are small and vulnerable.

tip
Don't place your chervil plants in the hot sun; make sure they are in a cool, partly shaded place and remember to keep the soil moist.

Chervil seed may take some time to germinate; sow in individual pots or cells and transplant to growing positions later. Be careful, though, as the plants do not like to have their roots disturbed. Alternatively, sow the seed thinly directly into your container; then, as the tiny seedlings emerge, thin them out, leaving space between them to allow for growth. The more space, the larger and bushier they will grow—I recommend about 8 inches between plants. For a guaranteed winter crop you can sow seed in late summer. If planting in a container, it may be easier to buy small plants to grow on—which will allow you to crop the plant sooner.

Planting in the fire grate

Here I have sown chervil seed into an old rusty fire grate and thinned the seedlings out so the plants have room to grow strongly. If you buy your young plants in pots, six plants will be enough for this size container. (Bought plants often consist of a number of seedlings in a single pot.) Gather the leaves from the outside of the plant, but pinch out the center if you see that it may be running to seed. Allow one or two plants to flower, as one of the most rewarding aspects of chervil is that it seeds itself liberally. These volunteer seedlings will become next year's crop. Leave them where they have chosen to grow, or gently transplant them while young. Do this after watering in the evening of a cool day, so they have the cool night to accommodate their new position.

Opposite Line the grate with a fiberous hanging-basket liner, cut to fit, and fill with a loam-based multipurpose potting mix before sowing seeds or planting young plants.

Indispensable basil in olive oil cans

you will need

empty olive oil can,
½ gallon or more

can opener

hammer

large, long, round-headed
nail

polystyrene tray for crocks

dibble

multipurpose potting mix

selection of basil
seedlings, such as sweet
basil and purple basil

I could not survive the summer without a host of bushy basil plants to use in the kitchen, and so I grow a number of varieties, suitable for different recipes. Luckily, you can now buy young plants, if not seeds, of differing types. I favor the lush Italian sweet basil for pesto and tomato salad; the purple, small-leaved Greek basil, less pungent in flavor but equally pretty, for use in salads. Lemon basil has a true lemon scent, and I will be growing this next year. My current favorite, Thai basil, has a strong aniseed accent and is an essential ingredient in aromatic Thai curries. I grow the beautiful large, shrubby African basil, with its purple-tinted leaves and stems and lilac flower spikes, purely for the pleasure of looking at it.

Opposite Basil planted
in olive-oil cans will
grow well on a sunny
windowsill or balcony.

1 Remove the top of the can with a can opener and hammer the edges flat, so that they are safe and smooth. Turn the can over and rest it on a firm surface, then make several drainage holes (five or six) in the base with the nail and hammer.

2 Break up the polystyrene tray into smaller pieces. Place these in the base of the can to help the drainage.

3 Fill the can with the potting mix, shake to settle it, and then add more, so that it reaches nearly to the rim.

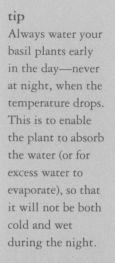

tip
Always water your basil plants early in the day—never at night, when the temperature drops. This is to enable the plant to absorb the water (or for excess water to evaporate), so that it will not be both cold and wet during the night.

4 Water the trays of seedlings. Using a dibble, gently remove a number of seedlings, trying to keep the soil around the roots. Place them in a saucer of water, to prepare them for transplanting.

5 One by one, lift the seedlings by the leaves, not the stems, and plant them gently in the potting mix. I have positioned the sweet and purple basil alternately. If you use a larger can, you will be able to plant more seedlings.

6 Finally, water the seedlings in; add more mixture if it sinks. Place the can in a warm place (a windowsill is ideal) and when the young plants are established and there is no more fear of frost, put them outside in a sunny position.

Anyone who makes their own pesto (and once you have, you will never buy it again) should grow a few pots of this marvelous herb. If you make pesto in the traditional way, pounding the basil leaves in a mortar with a pestle, then adding the olive oil, pine nuts, Parmesan, and garlic, you will release the intense aroma of classic Italian cooking.

Growing basil

Basil is happy growing in heat, but be sure to keep the mixture moist during the day. It will grow in a standard multipurpose mixture. I always grow basil on my sunny roof terrace, next to the tomatoes. They seem to belong together—both plants liking the same conditions. Basil is thought to have insect-repellent properties, so should help to keep the tomatoes free of pests.

Always harvest your basil by picking the young shoots out at the top of the plants before picking some of the lower, larger leaves; this will encourage the plants to branch out and will delay flowering, enabling you to crop the plant for a couple of months at least.

At the end of the season, allow one plant to flower, so that you can collect the ripe seed for sowing next spring. Keep the seed in a cool, dry place over the winter.

Sweet basil is really easy to grow from seed and is very rewarding, since you will generally achieve 100 percent germination if you have the right conditions. If you are not experienced at growing plants from seed, you may prefer to buy some of the more exotic basils as small plants, which will have been commercially propagated in heated greenhouses early in the year. This will give you an earlier crop.

Olive oil cans

In Mediterranean countries you will often see basil grown in reused olive oil cans, sometimes perched on a sunny windowsill. These containers are ideal, being large enough to hold the right amount of potting mix for a few basil plants. I buy always our olive oil in cans. Apart from being more economical than bottles, these cans often have attractive designs printed on them, and so are destined to become the new basil planters.

Above The blowsy green leaves of classic sweet basil contrast beautifully with the slightly serrated and more conventional leaf shape of the rich-toned purple basil.

A saucepan of chili and basil

Following the theme of planting basil in metal containers, I found this old enamel pan and loved the shape and brilliant blue color. Luckily, it had a rusted-through hole in the base and so I did not have to make one myself. I have planted it with a small chili plant, a Thai basil (because they are so often used together in cooking), and a purple basil, which I couldn't resist adding just for the joy of seeing it flower! It all seems a bit of a squash, but the plants will be fine so long as the potting mix is good. The occasional liquid seaweed or tomato food will be helpful.

If you don't want to grow chilies, you could grow a single variety of basil, especially if you use a lot in the kitchen. Three Thai basil plants would do well, or you could try the really lemony lemon basil.

A selection of various basils growing in a collection of old pots and pans not only will be useful in the kitchen, they will look beautiful on your terrace or balcony. When the nights grow colder, you could bring a few containers indoors to extend the growing season. They will be fine so long as they have enough light.

Above left Although allowing basil to flower will shorten its useful life, it is worth letting some plants do so. The flowers of all the basils are loved by bees. They have green or purple bracts, from which small round buds burst into pretty tubular flowers with extending stamens. Colors range from white to pink, purple, and lilac. When they flower, you will be sacrificing the culinary value of the leaves, which quickly become much coarser. You decide!

Right The saucepan is planted with Thai basil on the right, purple basil at the back, and a small chili plant on the left. All these plants were bought from a specialist herb supplier; they grow quickly and are soon ready to harvest.

Left These glossy little chilies will give an authentic fiery taste to a curry. Remove the seeds first to reduce the heat—or leave them in, if you prefer. Be sure to wash your hands immediately after handling the flesh—accidentally touching your eyes with unwashed hands would be painful!

tip
Harvest your basil leaves by pinching out the shoots and taking the leaves from the top first. New shoots will appear in the axils of the lower leaves.

Supermarket-rescue parsley in a box

I have always felt rather sorry for the live herbs that you can buy relatively cheaply in some supermarkets. The range has increased recently, and good supermarkets will sell most of the commonly used herbs, as well as some of the less common. The herbs in these small, crowded pots are grown intensively and are probably not organic; the flavor is generally weak and they are not what a good cook needs. They cannot survive long because there are too many seedlings in a pot.

Each year I have bought such a pot of basil, soaked it in water when I got home, removed the seedlings from the pot, and teased out the roots, separating the plants. These I then plant in a large pot of healthy organic potting mix,

you will need

large wooden box

pots of supermarket curly parsley (or herb of your choice; see overleaf)

rich potting mix (preferably with added well-rotted manure)

bucket of water

Opposite Once the transplanted parsley becomes established, it will go on producing fresh leaves throughout a long season. Parsley needs rich, deep soil, and the decorative and practical wine box makes a perfect planter.

1 Unwrap your pots of parsley and place them in a bucket of water so that the roots can draw up a good deal of moisture. This will help the plants to survive transplantation.

2 Fill your box with the rich potting mix, and remove the herbs from the pot. Gently tease apart the pre-soaked parsley, taking great care not to tear the fragile roots unnecessarily. Make a hole in the mix, deep enough to contain these roots without compressing them.

3 Plant the seedlings in their new home, either singly or in groups of two or three. Firm in well, spacing them about 4 inches apart, thus allowing them room to grow.

tip
You may notice some of the outer leaves turn yellow and die. This is not a problem—the plant is putting all its energy into making new, healthy leaves. Cut away the old ones to neaten the plants.

4 Water the newly planted herbs well, and place them in a sheltered, shaded place until they establish. You will know when this happens: they will perk up and stop flopping.

where I know they will have a long and happy life! They will not be chopped off and be allowed to dry and dwindle on the kitchen windowsill.

Recently I have started to buy other herbs and apply the same rescue techniques. The process needs care, time, and patience, but you will eventually be rewarded with a large and useful crop of healthy, flavorful plants.

Flat-leaf parsley works well; the curly variety, grown here in a large wooden box, is a little more temperamental but well worth trying. You do not need to separate all the seedlings: planting them in small clumps will be fine and less disturbing to the young plants. Parsley is a hungry feeder, which means that it needs a rich soil. You could add some well-rotted manure (if available) to the mix or feed the plants occasionally with a liquid seaweed mixture. They must not be in very hot sun, so place them in a slightly shaded position.

Using wooden boxes

If you can find a large wooden box, such as the one shown here, it will make an ideal container, since it will hold a useful amount of potting mix. If there are slits between the wooden slats on the base, cover these with a folded newspaper to prevent the mixture from leaking out. I found this box, originally used for shipping wine, out on the street for the recycling van to pick up; you might be able to get a similar one from a friendly wine retailer. Container gardening makes you very resourceful!

Right Flat-leaf, or Italian, parsley has become more fashionable than curly parsley in recent years. Its flavor is similar to that of the curly variety but more pronounced.

Boxed basil and mint

It is amazing that you can fill a good-sized box with just a couple of small pots of supermarket basil and make more than enough for one family to use (see instructions for growing parsley in this way, pages 50–53).

Greek basil is a small, bushy plant with a good flavor. The tiny leaves should be used whole, rather than torn, as you would use a larger-leaved basil. It is a little more sensitive than sweet basil and may take some time to establish itself in its new home, but once it does, it grows strongly and profusely.

Cultivating mint

Mint is a very easy option. I have planted it here in a discarded drawer (handle still attached!). These are often made of hardwood and so are durable. Two or three pots of mint are all that you need; it is a hardy, adaptable plant and looks good from the moment it is transplanted. Mint needs a lot of water and should be grown in light shade. Although it is a perennial plant, it will not be happy growing in a container in the second year: the nutrients in the soil will become depleted, and the leaves will lose the intensity of flavor. It is best to start again with fresh, new plants or take off the runners from the old plants to make new ones.

Remove the spent mint (that is, any growth that has lost its vigor) and plant directly in the ground, where it will recover its strength and flavor. Keep cutting the resulting plants so that they don't flower, which would make the leaves lose their freshness, tenderness, and intensity of flavor.

Which variety to choose?

Unfortunately, supermarkets sell just one kind of mint, and the variety is not usually specified; but from my experience the flavor is good and particularly useful for making a refreshing digestive tea.

This experiment with simple supermarket mint may inspire you to try some other varieties. There are some wonderful variants, such as chocolate mint, with its purple-brown tints on the stem and leaves; Moroccan mint for tea; and spearmint, the best all-purpose mint. I recommend a visit to a herb grower or specialist nursery, so that you can sample the wide variety of flavors and choose some to plant at home.

tip
The newly rescued plants will take some time to adapt to their new, roomier conditions. Keep their compost moist and protect them from direct sunlight until they have become properly established.

Right The dense habit of the compact Greek basil plants makes the planted wooden box look like a miniature forest. The mint will be happy in the recycled drawer so long as it can grow in a lightly shaded position.

Salads and coriander in a galvanized tub

you will need

medium-size old galvanized washtub

multipurpose potting mix

hammer

large nail

gravel for drainage

mixed salad-leaf seeds (cut-and-come-again)

coriander (cilantro) seeds

Ready-packaged mixed salad leaves with herbs are popular but rather expensive. However, it is very easy and cheap to grow your own combination at home in a container, producing enough leaves to have fresh salad a few times a week in the summer. This old galvanized tub is a good size, although once the potting mix is in, it will be too heavy to move, so plant it where you want it to stay. Salad leaves will tolerate some shade; in fact, the plants will bolt or run to seed if they are grown in the hot sun.

I have used a cut-and-come-again salad mixture, to which I have added some coriander (cilantro) seed. Plenty of salad mixes are available from mail-order suppliers and garden centers. Some are spicy and hot, with mustard and mizunas; others, such as the one grown here, are milder in taste. This one contains Russian kale, beet, spinach, arugula, and lettuce. Cilantro is often eaten as a salad ingredient, particularly in Greece and Turkey, and so it combines well with the other leaves.

Left This old metal washtub is bursting with goodness and flavor from a rich variety of salad leaves: red-veined beet, with its earthy taste; frilly Russian kale; peppery arugula; tender-leaved spinach; and the unmistakable flavor of that versatile herb, cilantro.

As the seeds germinate and grow, you may need to thin them somewhat, so that the individual plants have space to grow. They can grow fairly thickly, though, since you will be regularly cutting them for the kitchen. You will be able to cut your crop for just a couple of months, so if you want to extend the season, you should plant another container a few weeks later than the first. This second crop will then take over when the first one is spent.

If you go a week or two without cropping your salad leaves, they may bolt and flower and then produce seed. The flowers can be equally delicious—arugula flowers are a favorite with my family, having a nutty, peppery flavor. Cultivated arugula is best; it has pale cream flowers, whereas wild arugula flowers are acid yellow and very spicy. Coriander flowers are pretty white lace caps, with a delicate taste; the ripe seeds, which have a quite different, pungent flavor, are, of course, highly prized; these are extensively used in many cooking cultures from Asia to the Mediterranean.

1 Place the tub on a yielding surface, such as a lawn, and make a number of equidistant drainage holes in the base.

2 Add a layer of gravel for drainage, approximately ¾ inch deep.

3 Fill the tub with the potting mix until it comes ¾ inch below the rim. You will need to settle the mix (tamp it down) and add more so that it won't sink as it compacts.

4 Empty the packet of salad leaf seeds into the palm of one hand and sprinkle them evenly over the surface of the mix with the other. Then repeat with the coriander seeds.

tip
Salad leaves need some protection from the sun to stop them from running prematurely to seed; position the container to ensure this.

5 Sprinkle lightly with a thin layer of potting mix to cover the seeds; press down firmly with your hands.

6 Water the surface of the mix through a fine rose. Make sure the container is kept moist and out of the full sun; you could also cover the surface with a cloche to protect the seedlings and encourage them to grow. This is especially helpful when the seed is sown early in the season.

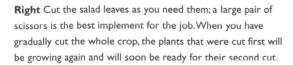

Right Cut the salad leaves as you need them; a large pair of scissors is the best implement for the job. When you have gradually cut the whole crop, the plants that were cut first will be growing again and will soon be ready for their second cut.

salads and coriander in a galvanized tub | **59**

Sorrel in a blue enamel tub

Sorrel is an unusual herb in having a sour taste. As a child, I used to pick the pointed leaves of the wild variety, which we called "vinegar plant," and chew on them. Sorrel is a perennial herb, much favored in France; the name "sorrel" is derived from the Old French word *surele*, meaning sour. A few tender leaves in salad add an interesting sour citrus flavor. Sorrel sauce, made with butter and cream, is excellent with fish; or you could add a few leaves with some plain yogurt to a rich, earthy beet soup just before serving.

The leaves of sorrel are similar to those of spinach; they contain similar quantities of oxalic acid and so shouldn't be eaten in huge quantities, though they are perfectly safe used as an herb. The buckler-leaved sorrel has a softer, more tender, shield-shaped leaf and is worth growing if you can find the seed.

Sorrel likes a rich, moist potting soil (add some well-rotted manure, if available) and does not like hot sun, so find a partially shaded position for your container. If you allow your sorrel enough space, it will make a large, long-lasting plant, which you can use as a cut-and-come-again herb to add to salads and other dishes. If you do grow it in this manner, crop the leaves regularly so that the new growth remains soft and tender. Cut the leaves with scissors when you harvest them; they will soon regrow.

tip
If you want to grow large, leafy plants, thin the seedlings in the tub so that about 8 inches remain between them. You will be able to harvest the leaves over a long season and may well have a crop in a mild winter!

Above left This attractive blue enamel tub can be reused as a roomy planter for the vigorous herb, sorrel. The plant will go on producing tender leaves over a long season.

Right The pale blue-gray of the enamel tub makes a subtle contrast with the soft green of the young sorrel leaves.

Fennel, caraway, dill, and coriander in fish boxes

Fennel, caraway, dill, and coriander (cilantro) are all umbellifers—a word derived from the Latin *umbella*, "sunshade." Their pretty flowers take the form of umbels: flat-topped clusters of "spokes" radiating out from the main stem, each having a tiny flower at the end.

Dill has been used in southern Europe and western Asia since ancient times. It was evidently highly valued: there are biblical references to taxes, having been paid in it. Today it remains a favorite herb of eastern Europe and Scandinavia. Both the feathery leaves and the seeds are used in cooking; the leaves have a milder flavor and can be added in large quantities. They are used in the marinade for gravlax (marinaded salmon), and pickled cucumbers are often flavored with dill (you may find a whole flower head in the jar alongside the

you will need

four polystyrene fish boxes (ask a fishmonger, who will be glad to get rid of them)

rich multipurpose potting mix, preferably with some added well-rotted manure

seed of four herbs: dill, fennel, coriander (cilantro), caraway

reed fencing

strong scissors

pointed stick for making holes (optional; see step 1)

ruler

Opposite These practical fish boxes have been wrapped in reed screening to tone down the whiteness of the polystyrene. When a few are planted together, they make an attractive "nursery" of young herbs.

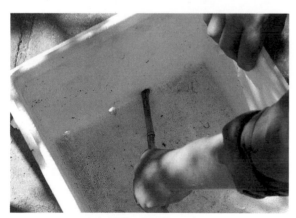

1 If the box does not have drainage holes, poke the stick through it at the base of the sides; you need about four holes along each short side.

2 Measure the height of the box and add 2 inches. Cut a length of the reed fencing to this depth, long enough to fit around the box, allowing a little extra. Cut through the reeds between the fixing wires at the right height.

4 Mix the well-rotted manure (if used) with the potting mix: about 1 part manure to 4 of mix—or about two handfuls of manure per box. Fill the box with the mixture up to the rim.

3 Wrap the reed fencing around the box. If it overlaps, remove the reeds individually from the wire weaving until it fits correctly. Don't cut the wire at this point. Join the reeds by twisting the weaving wire together. If you want the reed "sleeve" to fit more tightly, you can tie some garden twine or fine wire around the covered box.

5 Shake the box so the potting mix settles below the rim; if it goes too far down, add some more. Sow the seeds thinly over the surface.

6 Sprinkle some potting mix lightly over the seeds so that they are evenly covered. Press it down firmly with the flat of your hands. Put in a marker label so that you remember which seeds you have planted in each box. Water well with a fine rose, and place the boxes out of direct sunlight until the plants establish themselves.

pickles. The seeds, which have a more pungent flavor, are great in beet soup with sour cream. Dill aids digestion (its name may be related to the Anglo Saxon word *dylle*, "to lull"); because its effects are mild. It has long been used as the main ingredient in Gripe Water, a British medication used to calm babies with colic.

Fennel resembles dill in appearance, producing tall stems with feathery leaves and umbellate flowers, although if allowed, it will grow much taller—up to 6 feet. I have planted it here for its young leaves. We put a bunch of them, along with the crunchy stems, under a roasting chicken—the juices are delicious.

Coriander (cilantro) is an obliging herb. It grows easily, and—as with the others in this group—all parts are edible. The round, pungent seeds are widely used in Indian cooking, being ground into a curry mix with other spices. The fragrant leaves are an important addition to Thai soups and curries; being tender, they should be added only at the end to preserve the delicate flavor. We favor Greek and Turkish food at home and so use bunches of coriander leaves in fresh salads, as well as the cracked seed, cooked with lamb. I recommend eating the seed green; it has a fresher taste than the light brown ripe seed.

These three plants should be grown as annuals—meaning that you sow, grow, and harvest in one year. Caraway, however, is a hardy biennial: it will not produce seed until the following year after sowing. It is grown for this seed, which is widely used, particularly in central Europe, to flavor sweet and savory recipes, notably sauerkraut and red cabbage stewed with apples. It was a staple ingredient in the seed cake that I remember from childhood.

All these related herbs need basically the same growing conditions and can be easily grown from seed. Caraway and fennel will need the deepest soil to accommodate their long roots. To harvest seeds for sowing, wait until they are ripe (hard and light brown), then pick a stem containing a whole seed head, turn it upside down, and cover with a paper bag. When dry, store in an airtight container.

Using the fish boxes

Used to transport fish, these boxes are made from sturdy polystyrene, which has the advantage of helping to maintain an even soil temperature. They are brilliant containers for growing many herbs and salads; place a sheet of glass over them after sowing seeds to create a mini glasshouse—warm enough so that you can sow early in the season. However, the whiteness of the polystyrene is rather stark; to soften this, wrap the box with some reed fencing that you have cut to fit.

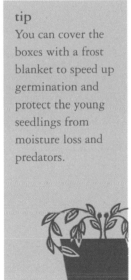

tip
You can cover the boxes with a frost blanket to speed up germination and protect the young seedlings from moisture loss and predators.

Above The first two leaves of dill and fennel are similar, so use a label to identify them.

Herb garden in a catering pan

Whenever I take things to the recycling dump, I come home with something that somebody else had no more use for, and I couldn't believe my luck when I saw these huge aluminum catering pans (another is shown overleaf) on the metal heap. I knew in a split second that, because of their size, they would make ideal planters for mixed herbs. It really is easy to convert the pans into planters (see page 38).

My everyday herbs

I used this larger one for perennial woody herbs: sage, rosemary, oregano, winter savory, and lemon thyme. These are my everyday herbs, which I need close to the kitchen. I have chosen to grow the variegated sage for its pretty leaves; the flavor is just the same as that of the various other sages and it is lovely to use with baked potatoes or pumpkin.

Rosemary is a beautiful, stately herb (its pretty blue flowers are loved by bees) with many uses in the kitchen. One of our recent favorite uses for it is to add the chopped leaves to some butter beans or chickpeas, along with garlic cloves and lots of extra-virgin olive oil; we then stew it all for half an hour and process it to make a delicious spread, which we eat on toasted sourdough bread. Oregano is perfect with beets and tomatoes; winter savory makes a great addition to French bean salad; and lemon thyme is a wonderful, adaptable herb, lovely with chicken or fish but equally good chopped in salad or baked with vegetables. You could add bay to this perennial mix, but because it grows large, I would suggest you grow it in a separate container.

None of these plants needs a very rich potting mix, but it should be loam based, as this retains the moisture better than a soil-less mix. In their natural habitat, around the Mediterranean, they grow on poor, stony soil in direct sunlight, which tends to make the flavor in the leaves particularly intense. All these herbs are evergreen, so they can be cropped year-round.

Above Sage is a really useful herb in the kitchen, with many more uses than just the traditional sage and onion stuffing. The leaves are pretty, too.

Opposite The herbs tumbling over the rim of this large catering pan will be happy for a few years. Trim them back when they become straggly and replenish the potting mix (add some new to the top) each season.

tip
Trim the herbs to keep them bushy and productive; you can do this a couple of times a year, in spring and fall.

Above Lovage is a tall herb with a big celerylike flavor, almost a stock cube in itself! We love to add it to soups and rice or grain salads. The old leaves are tough, so use only the young, tender ones. Cut the whole plant down in summer to encourage regrowth.

Center A lovely, rather underrated herb, chervil has soft fernlike, aniseed-flavored leaves, which are brilliant in an herb salad or lightly chopped and served with freshly boiled, buttery new potatoes.

Right Basil needs no introduction; grow it in large quantities for homemade pesto, or tear a few pungent clove-scented leaves over freshly sliced tomatoes.

Soft-leaved annual herbs

Here I've planted another catering pan (see page 66) with essential everyday, soft-leaved herbs. Most are annuals, meaning that they will not overwinter, but lovage will sprout again in the spring and chervil will obligingly produce leaves throughout a mild winter. I have planted the container with young plants, rather than seeds, in order to get an earlier crop; this is important if you want the herbs to coincide with your vegetable harvest. They will soon be overflowing and can easily produce more than you need, so you can give some away. Bunches of fresh home-grown herbs make lovely gifts—much more interesting than the ubiquitous bottle of wine when you're invited out to dinner! I make a delicious herb spread by adding finely chopped mixed herbs and garlic to a pot of snow-white quark (a kind of low-fat soft cheese).

These herbs will need a relatively rich potting mix, so you could add some well-rotted cow or horse manure (if available) or feed them occasionally with a liquid seaweed feed. Keep the soil moist.

tip
Picking these herbs
regularly will
encourage them to
produce new fresh
leaves. Lovage can
be cut down in
early summer; it
will then produce
lovely tender new
leaves, which are
the best to use in
the kitchen.

Left Summer savory is similar to the winter
version except that it has tiny pink flowers
instead of white ones—the bees love them.
The leaves are slightly more tender, but you
can use both varieties in the same ways.

Above With the right conditions you will
find that the herbs grow profusely, quickly
filling out the planter.

Parsley in a low Cretan bowl

Parsley is a staple herb of the kitchen. It is used in large quantities, especially in Europe—either fresh, in salads, dips, and salsas, or added at the end of cooking, in pasta sauces, soups, and casseroles. The flat-leaved variety grown here is my preference; although its taste is similar to the curly kind more favored in traditional British and American cooking, it has softer, deeply cut leaves. Parsley combines well with other herbs, such as coriander (cilantro), chervil, fennel, tarragon, and chives. For a delicious salsa verde, chop a combination of these finely, in a quantity to suit your taste or recipe, and add some extra-virgin olive oil.

This healthful herb is very rich in vitamins and iron and other essential minerals. It is also an effective breath freshener: chew a few delicious stems to sweeten your breath. I do this after eating raw garlic in a salad dressing—it really works.

you will need

large shallow Cretan-style bowl or similar, about 18 inches in diameter

polystyrene foam or pea gravel for drainage

multipurpose, loam-based potting mix

packet of flat-leaf parsley seeds

Opposite The beautiful Cretan bowl is overflowing with an abundance of healthy parsley leaves. Place the bowl near your kitchen door, as you will be paying it many visits to harvest the lush green leaves.

1 If you are going to place the bowl on a balcony or roof terrace, where weight could be a problem, add some broken polystyrene in the base to aid drainage. If the plants will be on ground level, you can use pea gravel instead.

2 Add the potting mix so that it fills the bowl right up to the rim. To make the compost richer you can feed the plants occasionally with a liquid seaweed extract to encourage healthy leaf growth.

3 Empty the packet of seeds into one hand, and sprinkle the seeds lightly over the surface of the potting mix with the other. The sparser the sowing, the less thinning out of the seedlings you will have to do.

4 Put some potting mix between your hands and sprinkle it over the surface of the pot so that all the seeds are lightly covered.

5 Press the surface of the soil firmly with your hands so that it is gently compacted; this helps to make sure the seeds are in contact with the soil and so aids germination.

6 Add a label and water the surface of the potting mix. Never let the mix dry out; check for moisture levels during germination. The soil should not be wet but should feel damp. When the seeds germinate and there are two real leaves showing, thin the young seedlings so that there is no less than 4 inches between plants.

tip

To speed up germination, you could soak the seed in some warm water for 10 minutes, which will remove a germination inhibitor on the coat of the seed. The seed may be more difficult to sow when wet, so allow it to dry out first.

I used to buy generous bunches of flat-leaf parsley in my local Cypriot shop, in London, but I soon learned how easy it is to grow. One packet of seeds, enough for two sowings, is more than you need to produce a year's supply of this healthful crop. The seeds take some time to germinate—even, occasionally, a few weeks—so you need to be patient. Sow the seeds where they are intended to grow, because the young plants hate being moved. Although parsley is a fairly tolerant herb, it doesn't like hot, dry conditions, so choose a lightly shaded position. Use a rich potting mix. The plant has long taproots, and so needs a fair amount of moisture.

Parsley will run to flower and seed in the second season; for a continuous supply you should sow some new seed early in the second year.

Pick the mature leaves regularly to encourage new growth, and cut out any flowering stems as soon as they appear to prolong leaf production.

To grow enough of this useful herb you will need a large container, deep enough for the taproots and wide enough to grow a great many plants. This lovely Cretan bowl—a traditional design that has been used by Cretan potters for centuries—is ideal. Luckily, this bowl is frost-proof, so in my relatively mild climate, I can leave it outside all winter without worrying about it cracking. Check the bowl you choose for frost resistance.

Pick the larger leaves from the outside of the plant, allowing the smaller central leaves to grow on.

Below The deeply incised parsley leaves are ready to cut when the plant is quite young; this should be two to three months after sowing the seed.

Lemongrass, chili, and Thai basil

With the widening interest in Asian cooking, you may find that you want to expand your herbal repertoire to include these three herbs, which are essential if you want to make any fragrant Thai curries. Luckily, they are easy to grow and widely available from herb nurseries as young plants.

Lemongrass, a tender perennial grass with a heavenly lemon scent, is a very common ingredient in Asian cooking. All parts are fragrant, but the swollen stem is where the citrus scent and flavor are mainly concentrated. If you grow the plant from seed (it germinates easily), it will take some time to build up this swollen stem. For this reason I recommend buying young, healthy plants from a specialist nursery. Lemongrass actually grows well when it is pot-bound. The container may look congested to you, but resist the temptation to transfer the plant into a bigger pot; it won't do so well.

If you look after this plant, it can last indefinitely. It likes warm and humid conditions in the summer and needs to be brought inside in the winter. As the days shorten it will become dormant (the leaves will shrivel) and you should water it only occasionally. When new growth appears in the spring, tidy away the old shriveled leaves and start to water again. You can feed lemongrass with a liquid seaweed feed every couple of weeks. It prefers a loam-based potting mix, and this needs to be kept moist.

Use the swollen stem to flavor Asian soups and curries. The tips of the grassy leaves make a wonderfully refreshing citrus-flavored tea.

Thai basil has an intense aniseed flavor and a wonderfully lush appearance. The leaves and stems are tinged with purple, and the exquisite small pink flowers emerge from purple bracts at the ends of the flowering stems. A member of the extensive basil family, it is less common than some varieties but is also easy to grow. Sow seeds and grow on in the same way as for sweet basil (see page 44). Harvest the leaves and shoots before they flower; this will also prolong the life of the plant.

Although chili is classified as a spice rather than an herb, I include it here because it is a close companion to lemongrass and Thai basil. Its intense, hot flavor is very important in Asian cooking. There are many varieties of chili, each having differing degrees of heat; it is up to you which you choose to grow.

Buying Asian herbs

I would recommend buying young plants, since you are unlikely to need very many. More adventurous gardeners might try growing them from seed, although this will need to be sown early in the year indoors because the fiery fruits need a long season in which to ripen.

All three plants are shown here growing inside on a sunny kitchen windowsill, where they will receive plenty of light. I have planted them in a group of brightly colored plastic pots, which suit their indoor position. The pots need not be large—a diameter of 6 inches and a depth of 5 inches are adequate.

Opposite This row of exotic herbs in colored plastic pots will brighten any sunny kitchen windowsill.

Right The red-tinted stems of lemongrass emerging from the blue pot—and just beginning to swell—contrast well with the pale green leaves.

tip
Keep the lemongrass warm and moist in the summer and dry and fairly warm in the winter.

Sages in long tom pots

Sage is a strongly aromatic plant, that can be used as both a culinary and a medicinal herb. The genus of *Salvia* (the Latin name, derived from *salvus*, meaning "safe" or "whole") is very extensive and includes beautiful herbaceous flowering plants, grown for their decorative qualities, as well as herbs.

Sage is a traditional herb to use with poultry—particularly in sage and onion stuffing. It also goes well with squash, onions, and potatoes and is often used in classic Italian cooking. Sage butter, in which leaves are crisped in melted butter or a mixture of butter and olive oil, is a brilliant sauce for gnocchi or squash-filled ravioli. Sage jelly, made with apples, is a great accompaniment to fatty meats.

In its medicinal role, sage is often used for colds and sore throats. Its well-documented antiseptic qualities make sage tea a common remedy for a sore throat (it can be made more palatable with a little honey and some lemon juice).

Growing sage

Despite its Mediterranean origins, culinary sage is really hardy, able to withstand fairly low temperatures without protection. The lovely purple or pink flowers are borne on long flower spikes; bees love them,

Opposite Planting two purple sage plants in identical long toms makes them suitable for a formal arrangement—either side of a door or at the beginning or end of a path.

which always endears a plant to me. A perennial, woody herb, with soft-textured leaves, culinary sage is evergreen, so you can harvest leaves throughout the winter (sage becomes rather musty and unappetizing when dry).

If you are growing sage in the open, let it spread, and trim the flowers when they have faded. If you grow sage in a container, trim it in the spring. The plant will eventually become leggy, and I recommend planting afresh every few years. Common sage can easily be grown from seed, but the broad-leaved purple or variegated versions should be propagated only by cuttings (see page 32). This makes it easy to create a few new plants each year—useful when you need to replace an older, woody version with a young, vigorous plant.

Long tom containers

Here I have planted two purple sage plants in identical long tom glazed clay pots (also called rose pots). Being evergreen, they will be decorative as well as useful herbs to grow beside the kitchen door. The pots need to be large enough to allow the herb to grow well, and you will need to use a free-draining, loam-based potting mix. The plants should not be allowed to become too wet in the winter, so do not stand the pots on saucers.

tip
Never prune a sage bush in the fall, because this can leave it open to frost damage. A trim in springtime should keep it in good shape.

The onion family

The onion family (members of the genus *Allium*) are very important in both the vegetable and the herb garden, contributing such useful vegetables as onions, shallots, leeks, and garlic, as well as culinary herbs, including chives, garlic chives, Welsh onions (similar to green onions), and wild garlic.

All have the most exquisite composite flowers; these are a dense collection of little florets forming a spherical whole. Leek and onion flowers, in particular, are absolutely loved by bees and many other pollinating insects. You sometimes see a number of different species around the flowers at the same time, all ignoring each other and all greedily searching the flower heads for the prized pollen and nectar.

For this planting I have combined two of the most useful herbs, chives and garlic chives, with two favorite vegetables: leeks and green onions.

Chives are the only member of the onion family to grow wild in Europe and North America. They have a mild onion flavor and are very useful in the kitchen, especially for flavoring soups, dips, and sauces. They are wonderful chopped finely

you will need

large metal wire basket

hanging basket liner

loam-based multipurpose potting mix

three wooden clothespins

dibble

scissors

plants: chive and garlic chive plants, a few green onions, and a few seedling leeks

Opposite This generous wire basket makes a perfect planter for members of the onion family. When the chives become untidy, just chop them off and they will soon regrow.

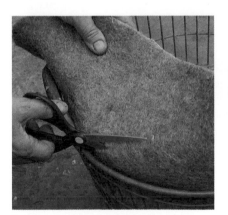

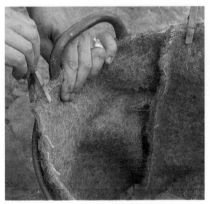

1 Place the liner in the basket and cut a piece to fit along the side, slightly overlapping the rim. You may need to cut a few pieces and overlap them.

2 Clip the liner to the rim of the basket with the wooden clothespins to hold it in position while the potting mix is being poured in.

3 Tip in the potting mix and fill to the rim. Give the basket a firm shake to help the mixture settle, and add more to reach the rim again.

4 Place the pots of herbs in a bucket of water so they are thoroughly soaked before being transplanted. Remove the garlic chives from their pot; make a well in the soil with your hands and firm in the plant.

5 These chives have been divided from a mature clump, as you can see from the tangle of roots and the small bulbils at the base of the stems.

6 Plant the chives 8 inches away from the garlic chives and firm in. Use a dibble to make holes approximately 2 inches deep in which to plant the leeks. Do not firm these in with your hands.

7 Plant the small bunches of green onions together, leaving a couple of inches between them and the leeks. Firm the soil around the onions. Water the basket well, making sure that each leek is watered in separately. Place, ideally, in a sunny position—although alliums will tolerate some shade.

with other soft herbs and garlic in cream cheese; we use this as a spread or on a baked potato. Chives form healthy clumps and produce small, globular, purple flowers throughout the summer. Like many other onions, they have tubular leaves. I grow chives in my vegetable garden along the path edges. When the flowers have faded, I cut the whole plant to the ground—they grow fresh and green again very quickly.

Garlic chives produce looser white flowers at the end of the summer. They have straplike leaves, which, as the name suggests, taste mildly of garlic. They are highly favored in Chinese cooking for use in soups and stir-fries, in which both the leaves and the flower buds are used. I love this herb for many reasons: it is pretty; it flowers late in the year— especially welcome when so many flowers have finished; it doesn't seem to be badly affected by pests or diseases, unlike some other members of the onion family; and it has a very neat growing habit.

I grow leeks not only for the table but also for their stunning flowers. They are biennial and will flower the year after the seeds are sown. You can sow them in May in pots or seed trays; transplant them when they are 6 inches tall.

Green onions grow quickly from seed during the summer. Sow in the same way as leeks. Alternatively, buy a tray of young seedlings and plant out as you would for leeks.

This group of four alliums will grow well in this generous wire basket. It has been lined with a feltlike material, the kind that is used to line hanging baskets, and I have used a good loam-based potting mix.

Chives (including garlic chives) will die back in the winter and will regrow again in the spring. Leeks will survive the winter and can be harvested then. Green onions need to be eaten as soon they are ready—just a few short weeks after sowing or planting out.

tip
Water the container thoroughly and regularly —the onion family needs a lot of water for the plants to thrive. Feed the plants occasionally with liquid seaweed to maintain their healthy growth.

Above The exquisite starburst flowers of garlic chives flower later in the season, after the purple pompom flowers of the chive plant are long gone.

Striped basket of rosemary

tip
Place a few rosemary sprigs on a barbecue, or use the stiff, woody stems as skewers for your grilled meat. The delicious fragrance flavors the meat and scents the air at the same time.

An evergreen, hardy herb, rosemary grows into a substantial bush with a very neat habit. The needle-shaped leaves, which are generally dark green with a pale underside and stem, grow tightly together and are extremely aromatic. The resinous fragrance reminds me of a cool pine forest, and it was this powerful scent that led people in earlier times to carry a sprig of rosemary or strew it on the floor, to ward off disease or mask a distasteful smell.

Rosemary's varied uses

Today rosemary has more positive uses, both medicinal and culinary. In cooking it is a classic herb to use with tomatoes or beans, on focaccia bread, and with roast potatoes and baked vegetables. A couple of sprigs infused in a bottle of extra-virgin olive oil makes a delicious flavored oil. We use this as a dip for homemade sourdough bread; it is so simple to make and delicious with a little sea salt and freshly ground pepper. Rosemary is a good herb to cook with lamb, as it helps to break down the fat in this fatty meat—an example of this herb's culinary and health-giving qualities working in tandem.

Among its other beneficial qualities, rosemary is antifungal and antibacterial. A few sprigs thrown into

Left Rosemary is a tidy plant—all the stems are upright, complementing the vertical stripes on the mauve and purple basket.

a hot bath will relax tired muscles, and I recommend the use of a rosemary massage balm after a hard day's work in the garden. Rosemary is often used as an ingredient in shampoos and hair rinses; it is said to make the hair shine. You can easily make a rosemary rinse by infusing a few sprigs in boiling water for an hour, then use the cooled water to rinse your hair.

Growing rosemary

Rosemary is easy to grow, although if it is grown in a container you may need to protect it from severely cold weather by putting some bubble wrap around the pot. Because it is evergreen, you can harvest the leaves all year round. It likes to grow in a sheltered position against a south-facing wall. You may choose to leave your plant to grow naturally and let it flower (it has lovely blue flowers in early summer and often flowers again in the fall), or clip it like a hedge or a piece of topiary; it responds equally well to either treatment.

I have lined this Mexican basket with an old potting mix sack, in which I have cut some drainage holes. Use a loam-based mix and don't overwater. As the plant grows it will need to be repotted into a larger pot. I suggest buying your first rosemary plant, rather than trying to grow from seed. It will grow quickly, and after a year or two you will be able to take cuttings (see page 32).

Marjoram and oregano in a metal tub

There is much confusion about marjoram and oregano, and it is not easy to explain the difference. If you consult a specialist book on herbs, you will find detailed descriptions of these plants, along with their Latin and common names, which will help you to identify them correctly. They both belong to a large genus called *Origanum*.

The tiny white flowers of sweet marjoram (*Origanum majorana*), also known as knotted marjoram, seem to grow out of a knot of tightly closed bracts. This is an unusual flowering arrangement and really worth a close look. The leaves are small, pale green, and highly aromatic. We use marjoram leaves at home—either fresh or in a sauce—with tomatoes, but we like them best on a cooked beet salad with feta cheese.

you will need

generous galvanized metal tub

large nail and hammer

gravel for drainage

multipurpose, loam-based potting mix

mixture of four or five marjoram and oregano plants, such as golden marjoram, sweet marjoram, Greek oregano, compact marjoram, and oregano

limestone chips and seashells (the latter optional) as mulch

Opposite Marjoram and oregano plants will gradually spread and grow over the edges of the tub. Once they start to flower they will continue right through until the end of autumn.

1 Using the hammer and nail, make about ten drainage holes in the base of the container (see page 58). Add an even layer of gravel about ¾ inch deep.

2 Add the potting mix, filling the container to the rim. Shake the tub to let the mixture settle, and add more to fill it up.

3 Make a well for each plant. Remove the herb from its plastic pot, gently tease out the roots, and plant it in the hole. Firm the potting mix around the base of the plant. Add the other herbs, spacing them at least 10 inches apart. For the most attractive display, plant the lower-growing herbs at the front of the tub and the larger ones at the back.

5 Finally, if you like, add a few seashells on top of the limestone chips. Although this is purely decorative, it is a good way to display a small holiday collection.

4 Add the light-colored limestone chips around the base of the plants so that the potting mix is well covered.

tip
Both oregano and marjoram can be dried, if you like, which is said to intensify the flavor. Pick stems on a dry day and hang them upside down indoors to dry. Strip the leaves when they are brittle, and store them in an airtight container.

Which variety to choose?

Golden marjoram (*O. vulgare 'Aureum'*) has bright golden green leaves, which form a mat in winter and grow into a dense, aromatic mound in summer. The flavor is similar to that of sweet marjoram, while the small leaves provide a variation in color.

The herb known as oregano (*O. vulgare*) has a much stronger, gutsy flavor—especially when grown in hot climates—compared to the more refined flavor of marjoram. Its profusion of tiny mauve flowers is irresistible to bees and butterflies.

Greek oregano (*O. heracleoticum*) has small white flowers and grayish, soft leaves. Its intense flavor is excellent for use on pizzas or in Greek recipes.

The flavor of all these herbs is similar, differing only in their intensity. I think they can be used interchangeably, without getting too preoccupied with which is which. I recommend growing several varieties of *Origanum*. Choose them for their growing habit, leaf color, fragrance, and intensity of flavor.

All these herbs are suitable for flavoring oils or vinegars. A stem or two immersed in a bottle of olive oil with an added crushed clove of garlic makes an interesting oil for drizzling on pizzas or tomato salads. It is also worth making herb vinegars, as they are expensive to buy. Stuff a few stems of oregano or marjoram into a tall bottle and pour in some heated white wine vinegar, then screw on the lid or insert a stopper and leave the bottle for a few days for the flavor to infuse the vinegar.

How to grow

These herbs will grow well in a container and are not fussy about the soil, so long as it is free draining, and they will be happy in full sun. I think it is best to buy plants and then make more, if you like, from taking cuttings in the spring or dividing the plants after they have flowered. This means lifting the plant out of the soil and cutting or gently pulling it apart to make a few more plants; the stems will pull away, bringing a portion of attached roots with them. Repot these new sections of the "parent" plant; they will soon establish and regrow.

This generous metal tub has been planted with a mixture of marjoram and oregano. It is large enough for four or five plants with differing habits; plant the smaller, spreading herbs at the front, where they can tumble over the edge, and the taller, more untidy ones at the back. The surface of the soil has been covered with a limestone mulch dotted with seashells. This stops the soil from drying out quickly, reducing the need to water so often, and has the added advantage of reflecting light and warmth up into the herbs.

Above Mulches can be decorative as well as practical. The idea is to cover the exposed soil to prevent moisture evaporating. The light tone of these seashells will reflect the sunlight and help to speed up growth.

CHAPTER THREE

Herbs for health

Herbs have always been used to aid good health, and in many cases they are extremely effective in treating common ailments. They are most commonly used to make digestive teas—most people are familiar with peppermint tea, and fennel has a pleasant aniseed flavor, especially when the fresh green seed is used. Coffee and black tea contain caffeine, a strong stimulant, and many people are now drinking more soothing herbal teas.

Lemon verbena is a shrubby herb that has intense lemon-scented leaves; it makes a pretty potted plant with lovely delicate flowers. Monarda, or bee balm, is a beautiful flowering plant, and the tea made from the scarlet flowers is a mild sedative. Chamomile, with its feathery leaves and pretty daisylike flowers, is well known for calming an upset stomach. All these herbs are beautiful when in flower, and it is rewarding to know that by growing and using them, you are continuing the ancient tradition of herbal medicine.

A teapot of apple mint

Surely the mint family is the best known of all the herbs—or perhaps the most notorious. Many gardeners would consider it not so much an herb as a rapacious pest that, if left to its own devices, will take over the garden.

But who does not remember from their childhood the subtle flavor of freshly dug new potatoes cooked with a stem of mint to flavor the boiling water, or fresh garden peas served with butter and a few chopped mint leaves? Mint jelly with lamb is a "must," and the homemade variety is far superior to anything bought from a store. My Swiss mother-in-law used to chop a mint leaf into salad dressing. We found it strange at first but use it often now ourselves, particularly on a cold

Above left This old brown enameled teapot is a witty and practical container for the most useful apple mint. Moroccan mint, grown for refreshing mint tea, has been planted in the green enameled bucket behind.

Above Apple mint is a commonly grown variety and is ideal for use in the kitchen. It has slightly gray, furry leaves and is a reliable plant. A sprig added to a pan of boiling water for new potatoes imparts a fresh minty fragrance.

fava bean salad with extra-virgin olive oil and lemon as a simple dressing. Mint figures prominently in the cuisines of many other countries, too. In Greece and Turkey it is combined with yogurt and cucumber to make tzatziki. It has long been used in the Middle East as a refreshing tea, mixed with a little black tea and a small amount of sugar. The popular Middle Eastern salad tabbouleh uses mint along with parsley, mixed with chopped cucumber and tomatoes and lightly cooked bulgur wheat. On the Indian subcontinent, mint is often used in sauces.

Mint's medicinal uses

Mint really deserves more attention, as it is a most useful herb. The powerful oil is used to flavor confectionery (think of chewing gum!). It makes an essential ingredient in antispasmodic medicine; in effect, it relieves indigestion and flatulence. It can also help to clear the nasal passages and relieve headaches. I rub or crush some peppermint or pennyroyal leaves on my arms and face when I am in the garden in the evening; it helps to deter the annoying midges and the preying mosquitoes. Altogether, it is probably the most useful herb you can grow.

Growing mint

An adaptable herb, mint is really easy to cultivate. It likes damp and cool conditions and will easily tolerate some shade. It grows well in containers but

you will need

old enameled teapot

hammer

long nail

pea gravel, ⅜ inch

soil-based potting mix

apple mint plant

1 Turn the teapot upside down and bang the nail through the base; this should be easy on an old pot.

2 Add a small quantity of gravel to the base of the teapot to aid drainage.

3 Add the soil-based potting mix, leaving enough room for the potted mint. You will need to move the soil around and up the sides of the pot so that it surrounds the plant when in place. Place the mint plant in a bucket of water for a few minutes so that its own compost becomes moist.

4 Tease out the roots of the plant so that they will quickly grow into their new home. A congested plant grows more slowly, as the roots grow around and around once they reach the confines of a pot.

tip
Allow some mint stems to flower. The beautiful mauve and lilac spires act as beacons for pollinating insects, which will fly long distances to find the enticing nectar.

5 Plant the mint in the teapot, pressing down and adding more potting mix if needed.

will, after time, lose its strength of flavor as the roots become congested and hungrily deplete the nutrients in the soil. If your container is small, either replenish the soil each season or, to ensure a fresh, concentrated flavor, put in new plants each year. Mint will thrive grown in the soil of a garden, but you may wish to contain its spread by first planting it in a plastic bucket; remember to make drainage holes in the base.

Mint varieties

There are many varieties of mint available, each with its own strength and characteristic flavor. Some have rather turpentine-like scents and so are best avoided in the kitchen. Eau-de-cologne mint has a rather intriguing perfumed fragrance, which might best be used by adding a few leaves to a hot bath.

The rule is simply to choose the mints that you like. With unfamiliar varieties (lemon-scented, for example, or ginger, chocolate, or orange!) rub a leaf gently in your hand and smell the oil before you buy. Most plant labels will indicate flavor and use in the kitchen, so follow that and your own sense of smell.

Right Silver mint (*Mentha longifolia*) shows a flowering habit typical of almost all the mints. The flowers, however, have beautiful, subtle lilac tones, while the leaves have the characteristic "furry" quality of some of the mint varieties.

tip
Mint is well adapted to container growing. Keep the mixture moist (a soil-based variety is best) and feed occasionally to keep up the nutrient levels. Don't grow the plant in full sun.

The mints pictured here are planted in two enameled containers: a green bucket and an old brown teapot, which has been much used in the past. The lighthearted reference to the tea-making properties of the pot's inhabitant makes this an entertaining project. On a practical level, these metal containers have the advantage of retaining moisture, unlike a clay pot, which would not be suitable.

Fennel in a chimneypot

Fennel is a statuesque perennial plant with feathery leaves and delightful acid yellow umbelliferous flowers. All parts of the plant taste of aniseed, with the seeds having the most intense flavor. In India these are used as a digestive to chew on after a rich meal; in Indian restaurants elsewhere you may be offered them, embellished with a layer of colored sugar. I often pick an unripe seed to chew on as I pass a fennel plant in my garden.

The rest of the fennel plant also makes a wonderful addition to many dishes—I couldn't be without it. We use the chopped-up leaves and young stems in salads and also place them under a roasting chicken (the resulting juices are delicious). Fennel seems to have some affinity with fatty meats,

such as pork, and of course it is well known for its usefulness in fish recipes.

Growing fennel

The common fennel grown here is often confused with the altogether "meatier" Florence fennel, which is grown for the bulb, or swollen stem. This is more of a vegetable and so needs a little more attention.

Green fennel is a stronger plant than the bronze variety of common fennel (see page 120), growing wider, taller, and more vigorously. They do look good together, though, and once established will make substantial, productive plants. Fennels like to grow in full sun, with fertile, well-drained soil. You could add loam or sharp sand to the potting mix to achieve this, and if it is grown in a container, you will need occasionally to feed your plants to keep up their vigor.

Fennel is easily grown from seed in early spring. Sow in pots or cell trays and plant out seedlings when they are still small, before they develop their deep roots, which don't like disturbance. Alternatively, buy young plants early in the year. Fennel will thrive only if the container is large enough to give the deep roots room. This is why I have chosen to plant it in this reclaimed chimneypot.

I have added some love-in-a-mist (*Nigella*) to the chimneypot because it combines beautifully with the feathery fennel, and I am a great believer in growing other flowers alongside your herbs. The flowers look great and have the added advantage of attracting beneficial insects. Actually, fennel is about the best herb for bringing in useful insects; parasitic wasps and hoverflies love the flowers, and their larvae can consume vast quantities of unwanted aphids.

Right If you grow fennel in a container, it will not grow as densely as a plant in open ground. Fennel has a lovely filigree habit that allows you to see beyond it.

tip
To prolong the leaves' cropping season, it is a good idea to cut fennel down to the base in early summer. It will soon regrow, producing many sweet immature shoots and leaves; these are the best to use in recipes.

Opposite The purple-tinged stem of the bronze fennel has a strange angular growing habit and is topped by the most wonderful explosion of acid yellow flowers. We use these widely in the kitchen for their wonderful, intense aniseed flavor.

Lemon verbena and lemon balm

Originally from Chile, this wonderful lemon-scented herb was imported into Europe in the eighteenth century by the Spanish. It is a tender perennial, woody herb, commonly grown as a decorative plant in large pots in Mediterranean countries, but it also has a practical function, as its leaves can be used to make a refreshing, fragrant lemon tea.

Growing lemon verbena

Lemon verbena will also thrive in northern climes, although it will need to be protected during the winter. That may mean bringing the pot inside to a cool room. It will drop its leaves, but these will re-sprout very late in the next season—possibly as late as early summer. You can leave it outside, wrapping the pot in burlap or bubble wrap, or use horticultural fleece which allows air to circulate.

I always plant verbena in a traditional clay pot: I like the contrast of the loose shrub, with its delicate lance-shaped leaves, against the beautiful earthy red of terracotta. Clay also has the advantage of allowing evaporation of moisture through the sides of the pot. This suits lemon verbena, because it thrives better in well-drained soil. The ideal conditions are warm and humid, so spray the leaves with a fine mist of water in the morning. Pick them throughout the summer and use them fresh for tea. They dry quickly and should be stored in an airtight container.

The leaves are often added to potpourris—try verbena leaves and fennel seed, or mix verbena with one of the gentler mints. These combinations also work well as teas. Being a sweet herb, lemon verbena works well with sweet food. I favor its use in ice cream and sorbet. It makes a lovely flavoring for a comforting rice pudding; just infuse the warmed milk with a few leaves before baking.

Growing lemon balm

Although it has a slightly less intense lemon fragrance and flavor than lemon verbena, lemon balm is easier to grow, tolerating shade and poor soil.

The ancient Greeks discovered that if you put a sprig of lemon balm in an empty hive, it attracts bees—its Latin name, *Melissa officinalis*, is derived from the Greek word for honey. As a bee keeper, I still do this to attract a swarm (it is believed that the queen bee's pheromone has a similar scent).

Buy a young plant from a nursery to start off. As with mint, you can pull off a stem and find small roots attached at the base; planted up, they will soon establish as new, bushy plants. For growing lemon balm in a container, I recommend the golden or variegated leaf varieties, which are prettier than the more common form. A loam-based multipurpose potting mix is best. Use fresh lemon balm leaves to make a tea; they lose their flavor when dried.

Left The exquisite, delicate flowers of lemon verbena appear in the early summer at the tips of the graceful branches. Remove the white and mauve flowers when spent, and the plant may produce more.

Left Lemon balm grows into a dense and fragrant shrub, which will spread rapidly around your garden if not restrained. It makes a lovely tea, with slightly less lemon flavor than tea made with lemon verbena.

tip
It is best to buy lemon verbena as a young plant, then, as it grows, repot to a larger-size container. Trim the plant in the late spring after the new leaves have sprouted. It will drop all its leaves in the colder months.

Left The more mature plant is growing in a classic Italian amphora-style pot. The smaller plant is happy growing in a long tom, but I will repot it into a larger pot next spring.

Aloe vera and houseleek

Aloe vera is a wonderful herb with well-documented healing properties. The sap that oozes from a freshly cut leaf, when applied to a cut or graze, makes a protective layer and then sets about aiding regeneration of the skin.

There are number of aloe vera varieties available to buy; the one shown here is *Aloe vera chinensis*, also commonly known as the Indian medicine plant. The best source is a specialist herb nursery. (Note, however, that the *Aloe* genus contains some 400 varieties, only some of which are medicinal.) Being very tender, aloe vera is most often grown (in northern climes) as a house plant. As it matures, it produces long flower stems surrounded by bell-shaped flowers, most often in a warm color: yellow, orange, or red. I would grow this plant purely for the fascinating flowers.

you will need

roof tile (with nail hole at top) with pots attached; alternatively, drill a hole in the side of two pots (see page 22) and fix them to a roof tile with nuts and bolts

two small pieces of a frost blanket (optional)

gritty potting mix

one small aloe vera, such as *A. vera chinensis*, and one small houseleek

1 If the drainage hole is rather large (as this one was), place a small piece of a frost blanket in the base of each pot to prevent the soil from leaking out. Alternatively, put a little gravel in each pot to keep the soil in.

Opposite This unusual planting arrangement is suitable for these succulents, as they need little soil—they store water in the leaves, hence the name.

2 Fill each pot with potting mix two-thirds of the way up; this leaves plenty of space for you to introduce the new plant.

3 Push the houseleek in place in the upper pot, removing some of the mix if necessary, so that the base of the plant is level with the top of the pot.

4 Plant the aloe vera in the lower pot in the same way. If necessary, add more potting mix around the base of the young plants. If the mix is slightly damp, it is not necessary to water them in.

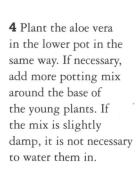

Aloe vera is a native of southern Africa; and although it will grow happily outside in the summer, it would not be happy in heavy rain. Always bring the plant inside in the winter, because the cold and wet would cause rot to set in, killing the tender plant. It is an ideal candidate for a cool greenhouse or sunroom, where it will flower in winter and early spring.

I have twinned aloe vera with a plant that has similar properties. Houseleek, more properly known as *Sempervivum*, can be used for healing: the sap of the leaves relieves stings, bites, and abrasions, although this quality is not well known. Unlike aloe vera, this is a hardy European plant. It is thought to have been introduced to the New World by colonists, and it has now spread worldwide. It grows commonly on walls and roofs, and being a succulent it needs little water to survive. Most recently there has been intense interest in these low-growing plants, which have been chosen as the main species for planting green roofs.

Both aloe vera and houseleek prefer gritty, well-drained soil. Here, both of these small plants have been planted in identical galvanized pots, which have been attached to a roof slate with small bolts. I bought this ingenious little planter at one of my favorite nurseries; they often have inventive ideas like this in their garden sundries section.

tip
Find a sunny wall or fence on which to hang the tile. Do not water the houseleek unless there is no rain for a while; the aloe vera will need a little more water but must not be overwatered.

Above The ruby tones of low-growing houseleek make an exquisite contrast with aloe's speckled tones. They enjoy similar growing conditions, although aloe needs protection in winter.

Large aloe vera in a pale clay pot

I have often seen bunches of succulent gray-green aloe vera leaves in African markets, and I used to wonder what they were for. It is only recently that I have several of this species growing at home—outside on my roof terrace and in my cold greenhouse—and have become familiar with their properties. I find these exotic plants fascinating, and although I have not had an occasion to cut and use the sap in the leaves, I would not hesitate to do so.

In the large specimen shown here (*Aloe vera barbadensis*), you can see the pale, grayish leaves all emerging from a fleshy central base, each leaf bearing a regular series of small spines along the edge. I have chosen a pale terracotta pot to echo the tone of the leaves. An added mulch of bleached seashells looks pretty, as well as having the practical advantage of reflecting warmth and light upward on to the plant.

I would not grow this plant from seed, especially since the mature plants produce small offsets all around the base, which can be removed, left to dry for a day, and then potted up in small pots to make new plants.

Always use a gritty, well-drained potting mix. I find that a clay pot not only looks good but also suits this plant, since it allows moisture to escape through evaporation. Bring the plant indoors in winter to keep it warm and dry.

Here, as on page 98, the aloe vera is shown partnered with houseleeks. These will thrive in similar conditions, although unlike aloe vera, they will happily remain outside all winter (to zone 5). Just make sure the pot is not standing in a saucer of water, as (like many other plants) houseleeks don't like having wet bottoms!

As a bee keeper, I am somewhat eager to try the healing properties of this plant. Although I try not to get stung (my bees are rather friendly!), I shall take some leaves with me when I next visit the hives, just in case.

Opposite Aloe vera is an ideal plant to grow on a sunny terrace or balcony, as it is well adapted to hot, dry conditions.

Below A few houseleek plants will soon crowd together, colonizing a decorative pot. Leave them alone; they do not need any attention.

Bottom A mulch of bleached seashells arranged around the base of the plant reflects light and warmth, enhancing the hot, dry conditions that aloe vera so likes.

Bee balm in a coal bucket

tip
Pick the flowers early on a dry day, lay them out to dry on a dish towel, and store them in an airtight container to retain the flavor and scent. Use a pinch of flowers for each cup of tea.

This lovely flowering herb is widely used to make a tea that has many beneficial effects. Although it is a native of North America, I first came across it in an Alpine village in Switzerland, where each small vegetable garden had a large, healthy clump of scarlet-flowered *Monarda didyma*, or bee balm. The narrow trumpet-like flowers were picked as they opened and were dried on dish towels in the sun.

The resulting tea, made simply by infusing the bright scarlet flowers in boiling water, is not red, as expected, but a pretty, clear shade of magenta. It is often used as a sedative and is said to calm the nerves and help one sleep. Other uses are to cure flatulence and relieve nausea. The tea is expensive to buy, so it is much better to grow it yourself. There are many varieties available, in various colors including pink, red, mauve, and white, but the best one for tea is called 'Cambridge Scarlet'.

The flowers open from the base of the compound flower, and so you can pick some new blooms each day. Just gently pull on each individual floret and it will easily detach from the main flower.

Bee balm is sometimes called Oswego tea, after the area of Oswego in the state of New York. In colonial times the local Native Americans used it as a remedy for colds. Consumption of Oswego tea by the colonists is said to have increased after they refused to accept British-imported tea, culminating in the Boston Tea Party (1773), when they threw more than three hundred chests of tea arriving from Britain into the harbor.

Growing bee balm

As its name suggests, this plant is absolutely loved by bees (it produces much fragrant nectar). It will grow in full sun but prefers moist, rich soil and a partly shaded location. Some varieties are prone to mildew on the leaves; although unsightly, this is harmless. If the plant is not too badly infected, you could just remove the bad leaves. It is best to buy young plants from a herb nursery or specialist grower; seed does not always grow well.

It is easy to take cuttings from the tips of the nonflowering stems in the summer (see page 32), but the best form of propagation is to dig up a mature plant in spring and cut sections of stem from the base with roots attached, then plant each of these in pots or cells. You will find that new shoots and leaves start to grow, making lots of new plants. The plant grows happily in a container; you will need a rich soil, which will retain the moisture that the plant needs.

Left The flowers of bee balm are really very interesting: the leaf bracts at the top of the stem are tinged with color and the florets grow like little trumpets all around a compound flower head. They mature from the base of the flower, while those at the top are still be in bud, so that the whole flower has a long life.

Below The galvanized metal coal scuttle, no longer used to bring in the coal, makes a useful, roomy planter for two varieties of *Monarda didyma*: 'Croftway Pink' and 'Cambridge Scarlet'.

Chamomile in a wire window box

Chamomile is a delicate but tough plant, which grows widely in unsprayed fields, on roadside edges, and on wasteland. Before the development of industrial agriculture, it was extremely widespread, often mixed among field poppies—making the cornfields appear to be dotted with red from the poppies and white from the chamomile.

Chamomile varieties

There are several types of chamomile, most having a characteristic sweet, apple-minty fragrance. The low-growing, nonflowering variety called 'Treneague' (see page 126) is the one you must use if making a chamomile lawn or seat. The double-flowered variety 'Flore Pleno' (see page 125) is very sweet-scented and is used more as a pretty ground-cover plant.

German chamomile is a wild plant, which is grown extensively as a medicinal herb. It grows taller than other chamomiles (in fact, it belongs to a different genus) and has many-branched flower stems bearing daisylike flowers, which are characterized by a deep yellow, raised, conical center. This is the type used to make commercially available chamomile tea.

Roman chamomile has its own beneficial qualities. More commonly used in a garden setting, it is known as the "plants' doctor," since it is said to protect neighboring plants from pests and diseases. The flowers are also suitable to use to make a gentle tea, which has a pleasant sweet taste and is used mainly to calm an upset stomach.

Pick the flowers when they are fully out, on the morning of a warm, dry day, and lay them out on a dish towel in the sun to dry; this also intensifies the flavor. When they are thoroughly dry, store them in an airtight container to preserve the freshness. To make the tea, infuse two teaspoons of dried flowers in a cup of boiling water and leave for a few minutes; strain and add honey and lemon to taste.

you will need

decorative wire window box, large enough to take three plants or more

hanging basket liner

scissors

multipurpose potting mix

three Roman chamomile plants

Opposite This pale green looped wire window box provides the perfect complement to the charming loose-growing habit of Roman chamomile.

1 Cut a piece of the liner to fit the base of the window box. Cut some more lengths the height of the sides, and lay them in place, overlapping them where necessary.

2 Fill the planter with potting mix so that it reaches the top of the liner. Shake the mix down, but don't add more as the plants will displace some of the potting mix.

3 Remove the plants from their plastic pots, tease out the roots gently, and plant them equidistantly in the planter. Firm in the potting mix around them with your hands; you can add more at this stage if necessary to cover the base of the plants. Water the plants in well and place the window box in its flowering position.

Right I have bought young plants from a specialist herb nursery, but you can grow this herb from seed. It will take a year for the plants to become large or mature enough to fill the whole window box. Sow the seeds in a seed tray following the seed supplier's instructions.

Chamomile is widely used in cosmetics, and because it has antiseptic and anti-inflammatory properties, you will find it as an ingredient in many gentle and soothing remedies.

You can easily make your own hair rinse (useful mainly for blond hair) by steeping a large handful of flowers and leaves in a pitcher of boiling water. Leave it for a few hours so that the herb imparts its properties to the water, and then use the cooled water after shampoo to rinse your hair.

The Roman chamomile plants seen here, planted in a pretty bent-wire window box, look lovely together even when the long-stemmed flowers wave rather untidily above the fine-cut fresh green leaves. Rub your hands gently across the plants to release a burst of sweet fragrance.

These easy plants love to grow in full sun and will thrive in a free-draining standard potting mix. They are fully hardy (to zone 4), needing only some protection in really freezing weather.

Right The waving stems of Roman chamomile look best against a dark background where the details of the many-petaled flowers and the feathery leaves are easier to pick out.

tip
Trim the plants back in fall, especially if they have become rather untidy. They will die back in winter, but will re-emerge in the spring.

Feverfew in a wire plant stand

Feverfew is a pretty herb, with deeply lobed leaves, which grows strongly and seeds everywhere—once you have planted it you will always have it! Although this longevity can be a welcome trait, you do not want to have too many offspring of the parent plant: they can grow large and take moisture and light from other plants. Feverfew is a herbaceous perennial, meaning that it dies down each winter and will regrow each spring.

Chewing on the pungent-scented feverfew leaves is known to be a remedy for migraines and headaches; however, the leaves have a bitter taste.

This can be disguised a little by placing them (two or three will do) between two slices of bread. I'm sure the remedy is effective, but I would prefer to take a feverfew tablet for my headache and forgo the leaf experience! (Also, chewing too many feverfew leaves can cause ulceration of the mouth.)

A better use of feverfew leaves, in my opinion, is as a moth repellent—something most households really do need, for the chemical alternatives are quite toxic. A few dried leaves in a muslin bag folded between your vulnerable clothes should deter those irritating, destructive moths.

Feverfew's daisylike white flowers, with deep yellow centers, are similar to those of chamomile, though more robust. They are borne in large clusters at the end of stiff, branching stems. They make good, long-lasting cut flowers and are wonderful in a country garden mix.

This herb grows easily from seed, although you can take cuttings in the summer from nonflowering stems (see page 32).

The pale-leaved or "golden" variety of feverfew is really pretty, but the plant is not so robust, and it will probably need to be grown with a little midday shade, as very hot sun can scorch the leaves.

Feverfew will grow happily in a container (use a loam-based potting mix) and will even thrive in quite dry conditions. Growing it in a pot will limit the eventual size of the plant. I have chosen to grow the common variety in a terracotta pot that has been selected to fit in this somewhat retro white wire pot stand. As a companion for it, I've chosen a golden feverfew, the lime green leaves of which contrast beautifully with the terracotta red of its hand-thrown long tom, or rose, pot.

Opposite Golden feverfew is smaller than other varieties and is grown for the color of the leaves.

Right The graceful lines of this 1950s white wire pot stand contrast effectively with the reddish tone of the terracotta pot.

Below Feverfew's cheerful white and yellow flowers appear in large clusters, and make long-lasting cut flowers.

tip
Feverfew seeds itself liberally; dig up the young seedlings and repot them to grow on as new plants.

CHAPTER FOUR

Decorative and scented herbs

There are many plants that can be listed in the category of herbs, including some commonly grown flowering garden plants. Lavender is probably the best known, with an extraordinary range of applications. It is used to scent potpourris, to repel moths, to make a refreshing bath, even to flavor desserts. Added to that, the purple haze of flower spikes in summer is loved by bees. Nasturtiums, with their strange round leaves and vibrantly colored flowers, are edible, the peppery flavor being reminiscent of arugula.

Pot marigold is known as "poor man's saffron" as it is used to color rice instead of its more expensive namesake. Pot marigold is the key ingredient in calendula cream—a miraculous healing ointment. I grow many herbs for their beauty and interest, rather than for their utility; for instance, I like to know that the essential oils of geranium or lavender are used in the perfume industry.

Lavender in a window box

Lavender is a commonly grown herb with quite exquisite qualities. On a sunny day, a large bush or hedge of lavender will be buzzing with swarms of greedy honeybees seeking out the nectar and pollen. I recommend kneeling down beside a flowering lavender bush in late June to take in the scent and the intense purple haze and watch the pollinating insects at work (they will not sting you—they have more important jobs to do). This is one of the great pleasures of gardening: allowing yourself these intense moments of pure enjoyment.

Fragrant lavender honey is a rare delicacy, much prized in France. Recently, some chefs have been using dried lavender flowers to flavor sugar, cookies, ice cream, rice pudding, jams, jellies ... an acquired taste, but interesting.

It is the scent of the flowers, which becomes more concentrated with drying, for which lavender is most valued. Its best-known uses are as an addition to a potpourri and as a filler for little sachets used to scent folded clothes in a drawer. As a bonus, lavender helps to deter moths.

Huge fields of lavender are grown in France and eastern England; these plants are grown for the valuable perfume and essential oils trades.

Left Lavenders look best when planted *en masse*, as a border edging or hedge or in a drift in an herb garden. In high summer the gray leaves are wonderfully offset by the brilliant purple flower spikes.

Right *Lavandula* x *christiana*—this variety is hardy only in warm zones (10–11), so must be brought indoors in winter. It has unusual three-branched flower heads and strongly serrated silver-gray leaves.

With its soothing qualities, lavender oil is often used for massage. Its many medicinal qualities (among them its antibacterial property and its effectiveness against stings and headaches), so well known in the past, are increasingly being recognized and again widely exploited today.

Growing lavender

Lavender is easy to grow. Like many of the shrubby herbs, it is a native of the Mediterranean. It will thrive in well-drained soil and is happy in a container in a sunny position. The plant flowers in midsummer, and so long as you cut back the flower spikes after they have finished, you will maintain a compact, healthy bush. Never cut into the woody stems, because the plant will not regrow from them. A second trim in early fall will ensure a healthy shrub.

You can sow lavender from seed in the fall, but it is more common to grow it from cuttings (see page 32), taken from nonflowering stems in early summer.

Now that there are many different varieties of lavender available in good garden centers, you may find it difficult to confine yourself to one type. This stylish modern window box has been planted with four different kinds of lavender. Growing them together helps to define the individual characteristics of each type, such as the narrow, fine gray leaves of one variety alongside the more unusual deeply cut, silver-gray leaves of another.

The flowers themselves vary in color and shape: note the unusual three-branched, deep purple flower heads of *Lavandula × christiana* against the burgundy bracts of *L.* 'Helmsdale'. Luckily, they will, at one point, all be in flower together.

Left *Lavandula angustifolia* 'Hidcote'—this is one of the most popular lavenders, often used as a hedge, since the plants are small and compact, with narrow, gray, aromatic leaves and intense purple flowers.

Below left *Lavandula* 'Helmsdale'—an attractive, unusual lavender, this has pretty ears of colored burgundy-purple bracts at the top of the flower spikes.

Right The anthracite-gray window box, which looks so modern, was designed in the 1950s by a Swiss architect. It has ingenious indentations at each end of the base to make it easy to carry.

tip

To retain the shape of the bush, remember to trim the flower stems after the flowers have finished. If you want to dry the flowers, cut the flower spikes in prime condition on a dry day, tie them in loose bunches, and hang them upside down in a dry place. You can, if you prefer, lay them on a cloth and turn them over as they dry.

Scented geraniums
in cast iron hoppers

Above These unusual cast iron containers enable you to grow and display lovely scented geraniums on a house or garden wall.

Geraniums are wonderful, rewarding plants, which are widely grown; however, few people are aware that they are also grown commercially for perfume and for distilling their essential oil. It is the leaves of aromatic geraniums that are scented; the flowers are often small and do not have any fragrance, although they can be very pretty. Allow the delicious fragrance

to stimulate your sense of smell: pick a leaf and roll it between your fingers as you sit outside or walk through the garden.

This is a huge group of plants (properly now called pelargoniums, but only by the experts!) with an extensive variety of leaf shape, color, flower form, and fragrance. I think the best way to acquire these lovely herbs is to visit a specialist nursery and choose a plant by its scent and appearance. Alternatively you could consult a catalog from a good herb supplier— one where you can trust the descriptions, as they will have been written by someone who really knows the plant.

Growing geraniums

It is easy to propagate more plants from cuttings (see page 32). In summer cut 4-inch-long shoots from a lower section of the plant where there is no flower bud. Cut off the lower leaves and push the shoots into a gritty seed-starting mix, positioning them around the edge of a plastic pot. Keep the mix moist but definitely not wet (geraniums can succumb to rot if they get too wet). They should root rapidly, in a matter of weeks. Once they have strong roots, pot them on into individual pots containing a general-purpose potting mix. As they grow, pinch out growing tips to make the plant bush out into a compact shape.

Geraniums are some of the easiest plants to look after—and perhaps the most adapted to growing in containers. They are traditionally grown in terracotta pots, but so long as they are grown in a warm, sunny place, they will be happy. Watch out, though: you can't leave them outside in winter and so will need a roomy windowsill on which to keep them all.

These old cast iron gutter hoppers make excellent planters. They have convenient flat backs, with lugs that allow them to be fixed to the wall easily, and they are large enough to hold sufficient potting mix to nourish the plant. You will need to put something into the base of the hopper (where the downspout would have been attached) to stop the

Above This pretty geranium, with its finely cut, lime green leaves, has charming little pink flowers, which will perform all summer.

mix from leaking out. A scrunched-up plastic bag will serve this purpose. Use a loam-based potting mix, which will retain moisture. Feed the geranium with a liquid seaweed extract when the first flower buds appear and thereafter weekly.

Geranium leaves are never eaten; instead, they are used to lend fragrance to a sweet dish. A leaf at the base of a pot of clear crab-apple jelly gently imparts its fragrance over time. Wash and dry the leaf first; then place it at the base of the jar, pour the hot jelly over and seal in the normal way.

> **tip**
> It helps to deadhead the flowers as they fade to make way for new ones. If you are a very tidy gardener, you may wish also to remove the old brown or damaged leaves.

Pink tub with red-leaved herbs

All the stunning deeply hued herbs growing in this vibrant pink container are grown for their startling color and sheer bravado. They are all edible but perhaps would not be everyday staples!

Fennel is perhaps the best known of these and the most widely grown; the bronze variety, planted here, grows less strongly than the more common green (see page 94). Its flat, decorative yellow flowers attract insects of all kinds, especially hoverflies and parasitic wasps. No garden should be without these, since they are nature's natural pest control, eating copious numbers of aphids. Fennel seeds are really useful in the kitchen and are commonly used for cooking in many cultures. The ripe seeds make a lovely digestive tea, particularly if you bruise them slightly with a mortar and pestle before adding boiling water.

The perilla, sometimes called Chinese basil, is grown mostly for its stunning purple leaves. It is a popular herb in Japanese cooking, where the green variety is more generally favored; but you will find only the most adventurous Western chefs using the young leaves. I grow it decoratively because it is unlike any other

you will need

large plastic (or rubber) garden tub, about 14 inches high and 16 inches in diameter

craft knife

pea gravel for drainage (or use broken-up polystyrene as a lighter alternative)

multipurpose potting mix (with added perlite to lighten the mix—helpful when planting on a roof terrace or balcony)

one fennel, one red sorrel, three red orache, and one perilla (young plants)

Opposite The bright pink ribbed container sets off the vibrant reds and pinks of the decorative herbs it contains. This color may also echo some early summer pinks elsewhere in your garden.

1 Cut a number of small holes in the base of the container using the craft knife. It is easiest to cut three straight lines in the form of a triangle and then push out the center.

2 Cover the base with approximately ¾ inch of gravel to act as drainage.

3 Fill the container with the multipurpose mix; shake to allow it to settle, then add some more. Place young plants in a bucket of water before planting them out; this allows the roots to draw up water, helping the plants to acclimatize to new conditions.

4 Take the plant (here fennel) in one hand, holding the leaves and stem carefully between your fingers, then remove the pot with the other hand.

5 Plant each herb in the potting mix, first making a well in it with your hand and then firming the plant in place. Position the sorrel and perilla equidistantly from each other and the fennel.

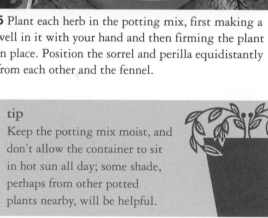

tip
Keep the potting mix moist, and don't allow the container to sit in hot sun all day; some shade, perhaps from other potted plants nearby, will be helpful.

6 Plant the young orache plants in the gaps between the other herbs. Water the plants gently.

herb. Although it can be confused with basil 'Purple Ruffles', when you look carefully at the perilla leaves, you will notice a gasoline-like iridescence, which is uncommon in the plant world.

Red-veined sorrel adds a contrast in form, as it is a low-growing, spreading plant. If you want to use the vinegary taste of sorrel in your cooking, I suggest the more common green variety or the buckler-leaved sorrel (see page 60); however, the young leaves add an interesting sour taste to a mixed salad.

Red orache, a fabulous ornamental herb, is an almost luminous fuchsia pink when young, especially with the sun behind the leaves. It grows into a tall and graceful plant, providing an unusual color accent in the garden throughout the year. Small young leaves can be eaten raw in salads, to which they will add a truly exotic color; the older leaves, which have a more earthy, yet gentle flavor, are more commonly eaten like spinach (though not at my table—I prefer spinach). Leave orache to grow naturally and allow it to self-seed, which it does generously everywhere!

Choosing your container

There is no reason why your chosen container can't be as colorful as the herbs you grow in it. This pink plastic tub is a very useful and inexpensive piece of garden equipment; I have a variety of them in different colors and sizes. I use them to collect

vegetables, to gather materials for the compost pile, and to carry soil, water, and mulches.

I have now added another use for them: as perfect planters. The tough, lightweight plastic material makes them ideal for use on balconies and roof gardens, and the handles make them easy to move around. The nonporous material prevents the loss of water through evaporation; you need only cut a few drainage holes in the base.

Below The unique carmine leaves of orache seem to glow when the light shines through them. Although the flowers are rather insignificant, it's a good idea to let them bloom so that they can set seed for next year.

tip
If you would like the orache to become a bushier plant, pinch out the growing tips to encourage more side growth to develop.

Catnip in an inviting basket

This is a project for all the cats out there! They can indulge in the heady delights of *Nepeta* (the Latin name for catnip, or catmint) to their hearts' content in this generous wicker basket and then fall into a delightful stupor—it's a sort of cat basket with an added extra! All parts of the plant are irresistible to cats (though a few cats are unaffected by it), especially when it has recently been handled. This brings out the scent, which contains a property that cats confuse with a pheromone from a cat of the opposite sex. A cat that discovers some newly planted catnip can almost destroy it with its amorous intentions! We always give our cats Christmas presents of little fabric mice stuffed with dried catnip leaves—it keeps them amused for hours.

Mere humans are generally impervious to the scent of catnip (though the dried plant is said to have mild hallucinogenic properties when smoked), and I am not fond of it. However, the plant has plenty of other attractions for the gardener. A loose, tumbling herb, it bears a profusion of blue/purple flowers and gray-green crinkly leaves, similar to sage, and it is much used along the edges of borders, where it can spread across and soften the edges of a garden path. I love to use the long blue flower stems in blowsy bunches of summer flowers; they look lovely combined with frothy, lime green alchemilla flowers and old English roses.

This is an easy herb to grow, and you will find that it will flower from late spring until early fall.

Far left This charming double-flowered chamomile is happy growing at the edge of the basket.

Left The pretty lilac-blue flowers of catnip are studded all along the length of the trailing shoots. They are a magnet for bees and other pollinating insects.

Right This low, wide basket makes a perfect planter for the tumbling habit of catnip, and it also makes for easy access for cats of all ages!

It does help if you trim the whole plant back in midsummer in order to stimulate new growth and more flowers.

Making a catnip basket

You will first will need to line the basket with an empty potting mix sack, making a few slits in the base of the sack for drainage. It is best to use a loam-based mix, which helps retain moisture. In this basket I have planted two catnip plants, both *Nepeta racemosa* 'Walker's Low'. Do not plant more—they spread and ramble rather quickly, so they do need plenty of space to expand. I have tucked a double-flowered chamomile into one corner, so that it tumbles over the edge, and also a silvery-leaved tansy.

It is best to buy young plants, rather than sowing seed; they quickly grow into mature ones, and you can divide these the following year to make more plants. It is also possible to take softwood cuttings (see page 32) from new shoots in early summer. Treat these in the same way as lavender cuttings. Catnip is a hardy, long-lived herb. Cut the plant back in winter and mulch with straw or a light potting mix as a protection from frost.

Colanders with pennyroyal and chamomile

you will need

two spacious kitchen colanders

sphagnum moss (as used for lining hanging baskets)

loam-based multipurpose potting mix

water-retaining granules

one pennyroyal plant

one 'Treneague' chamomile plant

Both pennyroyal and 'Treneague' chamomile (a non-flowering variety) are powerfully scented herbs. They are low-growing, which makes them ideal for planting along the edges of a garden path, so that as you brush past or tread gently on them they will release their wonderful scent.

I grow pennyroyal because I love its intense peppermint fragrance—and I do mean intense, like extra-strong mints! Sometimes a plant needs to stimulate only one of your senses to earn a place in the garden. But pennyroyal is also a decorative plant: when it flowers, it produces tiny whorls of lilac-colored flowers around the upright stem.

I often garden in the evening, which is unfortunately when the biting insects are around. To repel them I crush a sprig of pennyroyal onto my bare skin.

Opposite If you place these two verdant colanders on an outside table, you won't be able to resist rubbing your hands across them to release the spectacular fragrance.

1 Line the colanders with a layer of sphagnum moss, so that the metal surface is well covered. Immerse the potted plants in a bucket of water to moisten their roots.

2 Add some water-retaining granules to the potting mix, using the scoop provided and carefully following the manufacturer's instructions. I wear gloves when handling the granules, just for reasons of hygiene.

3 Add the potting mix to the colanders, leaving about an inch free around the rim; this is to allow space for the excess potting mix dug out to make room for the plants.

4 Make a well in the potting mix and plant the chamomile, first gently teasing out the roots. Position the plant in the middle of the colander, so that it will creep outward and eventually flow over the rim. Firm it in gently, adding more mix if needed.

5 Plant the pennyroyal in the other colander. Add more mix to both plants if necessary to build up the level, then water them well.

tip
Crush some fresh leaves of pennyroyal to release the intense peppermint scent, and rub them over bare skin to act as an insect repellent.

The fragrance is a lot nicer than some store-bought insect repellents, although I wouldn't say it is 100 percent effective as a deterrent. However, the sap rubbed on a bite will help to relieve itching. In the past, an infusion of pennyroyal leaves was used to ease cold symptoms. Curiously, the essential oil extracted from this herb is rather toxic and should not be used.

'Treneague' chamomile is most commonly planted as a lawn or seat. The fernlike leaves are dense, and it makes a springy mat with the loveliest fragrance. Describing the fragrance of herbs is quite challenging because they are often only like themselves! This chamomile is sweet and rich, with mild mintlike undertones; just rubbing your hand across it as you pass by is a rich pleasure.

I have planted both these herbs in old metal colanders. I love these domestic containers and have quite a collection. Most often I use them for collecting fruit and veggies from the garden, but I thought these two low-growing, spreading herbs would grow well in them. The plants could be placed by the back door, or on a garden table, so that you could run your hands over them to release their spectacular scent as you sit with your morning coffee.

Both plants will grow happily in sun or partial shade, but they do like a good potting mix and must be well watered. I have suggested adding water-saving granules to the mix since the containers are small and the mix could dry out rather quickly.

Above right I love the circular pattern of punched holes in the dull aluminum colander. The pennyroyal will gradually creep over the rim.

Right The feathery leaves of the 'Treneague' chamomile will eventually tumble over the edge of the colander, making a green curtain.

Birdcage of nasturtiums

Once you sow nasturtium seeds, you may never need to do so again. These plants are prodigious self-sowers and will pop up in any spare soil. Although this can be a nuisance, they are easy to pull out if they appear in the wrong place. Luckily, they will grow well in pots and other containers.

These tender, half-hardy annuals fall into two distinct groups: trailing, which can also climb untidily (they can travel a long way!), and compact nasturtiums, which are better behaved. Native to South America, they come in a fantastic range of rich, warm colors, from peachy pink to deep orange and mahogany red. The flowers are an extraordinary shape: five-petaled with a hooked tail behind. The leaves are unusually round, with the stem attached from behind, which makes them look like little dishes; it is wonderful to see a drop of pearly dew resting in the center early in the morning. These leaves can be acid green

you will need

decorative birdcage or similar

hanging basket liner

scissors

multipurpose potting mix, mixed with loam or garden soil

six or seven nasturtium seedlings, two kinds

two or three arugula seedlings (optional)

Opposite Nasturtiums come in such a range of vibrant colors, from deep, fiery red to the palest yellow, via all shades of orange.

1 Stand the birdcage on the hanging basket liner and cut around it, leaving a margin of approximately 6 inches.

2 Make a series of 6-inch inward cuts around the circle of liner. Open the top of the cage and place the liner in the base; fold the cuts up the sides, overlapping them so that there are no gaps for soil to escape through.

3 Tip your potting mix into the lined base, and fill so that it reaches to the top of the liner.

4 Take your seedlings and plant them equidistantly in the potting mix. Plant some through the wire walls of the cage to encourage these to grow outward.

5 Plant a few arugula seedlings in the gaps between the nasturtiums.

6 Make sure that all the young plants are firmly planted, then add some more potting mix so that all the roots are covered. Water and place in a protected position until the plants have become established— this takes a few days. Then hang the birdcage in its flowering position.

tip
Make sure the potting mix remains moist; this is important because nasturtiums are happiest when grown in full sun and the soil will dry out quickly.

or glaucous blue-green; there are even blotched and variegated kinds.

Nasturtiums are perfect companion plants and are often grown sacrificially by vegetable gardeners —that is, to lure black flies and cabbage white butterflies away from brassicas and fava beans. The open flowers attract hoverflies, the larvae of which attack aphids, while the strong scent deters other pests. Altogether it is a most useful plant!

Besides being beautiful, easy to grow, and useful, nasturtiums are even completely edible. In fact, some major supermarkets are selling the flowers as salad ingredients. The leaves (and to a lesser extent the flowers) taste peppery; a few leaves or flowers tossed into a mixture of salad leaves makes a spectacular summer dish.

Nasturtiums prefer a poor soil, which means you can mix some garden soil or loam into your potting mix when planting in containers. Never feed, as this will stimulate the plant to produce all leaf and no flowers.

This pretty wire birdcage makes an unusual planter for some compact nasturtiums. It is much nicer than a conventional hanging basket, although the growing conditions are the same and you need to look after it in the same way.

Below This variety has pale yellow flowers with bright orange blotches and is just one example of the huge range of colors available when you buy nasturtium seeds.

Pinks in a woven basket

The original wild pinks (*Dianthus* species) are pink! The origin of the name "pink" is uncertain, but I like to think it comes from the serrated rim of the petals, which look as if they have been cut with pinking shears. (Or it could be that pinking shears are named after pinks!) The many cultivars come in many shades of pink and red, as well as white. I prefer the single varieties, although some of the double flowers can be very pretty.

The outstanding characteristic of this plant is the exquisite scent—a powerful, spicy fragrance reminiscent of cloves—hence the alternative name "clove pink."

you will need

small, colorful basket

plastic bag: red or pink to match basket

scissors

multipurpose potting mix with added loam

fine gravel (optional)

two *Dianthus* plants with different colors and petal markings

Opposite There is a veritable explosion of vibrantly colored, sweetly scented pinks in this charming Mexican basket. It would make a perfect present for a child who loves gardens and flowers.

1 Place the plastic bag in the basket and cut off most of the excess, leaving approximately 4 inches above the rim of the basket.

2 Remove the plastic bag from the basket and cut a few small snips in the base of the bag to act as drainage holes.

3 Replace the bag in the basket and fold the edges down so they are level with the rim of the basket. You can adjust this again later once the potting mix is in.

4 Blend the potting mix well, adding some fine gravel if you are using a large container. Fill the basket until the mix reaches the rim; this will settle later.

5 Using your hand, make a planting hole in the soil at one end of the basket, and insert one of the plants. Plant the other at the opposite end, firming the soil down as you go.

6 Add more potting mix around the plants, taking care not to cover the base of the plant too much. Gently water the newly planted pinks and place the basket in its chosen position.

Not many people will know pinks as an edible herb, but they have long been used in this way. Only the petals are used; they need to be detached from the flower, and the bitter heel needs to be removed to make them palatable. The petals are best used in puddings and other desserts or to flavor jam and cordials. Arguably, the best treatment is to crystallize the petals and use them to decorate cakes, as one would use crystallized violets or rose petals. Whether or not you choose to eat pinks, I think it is good just to know that you *can* eat them. Knowing about the history and properties of a plant tends to make its cultivation so much more interesting.

Personally, I would follow the Roman and Greek tradition of weaving the beautiful, fragrant flowers into wreaths and garlands, and consume them only on a very special occasion—perhaps to decorate a big bowl of fruit salad, along with violas and borage.

Growing pinks

Pinks are really wonderful small plants. They are extremely hardy (I have seen them growing wild high in the Alps, where the winters are very harsh), and if you give them plenty of sun and well-drained soil they will reward you with a long and prolific flowering season.

This plant is evergreen (a valuable asset in a small garden), and the low-growing rounded mat of gray-green leaves looks good throughout the year, even without the flowers. Pinks are adaptable plants and are happy growing in containers. This brightly colored child's plastic basket suits them perfectly. You just need to make sure that the potting mix is loam-based. You can add some fine gravel or sharp sand to aid drainage, although there shouldn't be a

Above Look closely at the flowers—the petals have pretty markings on them, often with a deeper-colored center.

problem in such a compact container. Avoid overwatering the plants.

It is easy to take cuttings from pinks—tip cuttings in spring or heel cuttings in early fall. The latter are perhaps easier: just pull a shoot away from the main stem, leaving a small heel at the base; strip away a few leaves and push them into gritty seed-starting mix. Do not overwater. Alternatively, take layered cuttings in spring from a stem that has produced roots along the length where it has been in contact with the soil.

tip
Be sure to remove the wilted flowers (deadhead) to extend the flowering period. The plant will then produce flowers from lower down the stem.

tip
Deadhead the flowers regularly to extend the growing season. Pick fresh flowers for culinary or medicinal use in the morning on a dry day.

Left This jazzy Mexican basket has been chosen to match the vibrant orange and yellows of the pot marigolds.

Opposite On this opening bud of an 'Indian Prince' marigold, you can see the bronze reverse side of the orange petals.

A basket of pot marigolds

This cheerful, easy-to-grow flower—planted here in a bright Mexican basket with some perky violas as a contrast—is "not just a pretty face;" in fact, it's one of the most useful herbs you can grow.

Native to Europe and Iran, pot marigolds have been dubbed the "poor man's saffron." Although not having as intense a flavor or color as saffron, they nonetheless can be used in the same way, to color rice, milk, or cakes. A few petals are a fine addition in a salad, perhaps along with a couple of peppery nasturtium flowers and leaves.

Marigold's uses

The flowers have really effective antiseptic and antifungal properties, and so the plant has many medicinal uses. You may be familiar with its Latin name, *Calendula officinalis*. (True marigolds belong to the *Tagetes* genus.)

I use calendula cream in place of any other antiseptic cream for small injuries and abrasions, and

I swear by it. It is also commonly used in cosmetics: for lotions, hand creams, and shampoos.

So you see, this is one herb that you could use to make your own home preparations, and it has the advantage of being very easy to grow. Sow seeds once and you have it in your garden forever, for it self-seeds prolifically. No gardener minds this—it is a perfect companion plant, as it attracts beneficial insects. It even tells you the weather: the flowers open and close with the sun!

Growing marigolds

There are many cultivars of the pot marigold that are worth growing; look at seed packets to choose the color tones that suit you. I really love one called 'Indian Prince', which has bronzy undersides to the petals. You can sow seed in fall in the ground where you want the plants to flower. Or, if you want to grow them in containers, it is better to sow the chunky seeds in the spring in small pots and then transfer them to the chosen position. If you like, you can pinch out the center of the growing tips to make a bushy plant; however, I never do this as I prefer them to grow rather untidily.

To grow them in a plastic basket, such as this one, see the instructions on pages 135–136. A normal multipurpose potting mix will do. You can squash a number of plants into a large basket, but just a few will grow larger and produce flowers over the length of the summer.

Pineapple and blackcurrant sages

In addition to the purple sage shown on page 76, I grow two other aromatic sages each year. I don't use the leaves; I just love to brush past them to release the magical fragrance. And I absolutely love their delicate profusion of flowers—as do bees and other pollinating insects.

Pineapple sage is a vigorous, bushy plant, which needs to be planted fresh each year, as it will not tolerate cold weather (although it is a perennial and could survive inside on a sunny windowsill). Its leaves smell sweetly of pineapple, and in late summer it bears a mass of long, tubular-shaped scarlet flowers. It grows fast and needs a roomy planter, such as the generous galvanized bucket shown here. As with any sage, the soil should be loam-based and free-draining. Don't feed until after the plant has flowered, or you will get a profusion of leaves at the expense of the flowers. This sage is a native of Mexico, where its nectar is reputed to be highly favored by hummingbirds. In Britain we have to be satisfied with frequent visits from our industrious bees!

Blackcurrant sage is a rather loose and untidily growing herb. The small, dark green leaves smell strongly of blackcurrants (*Ribes nigrum*), and the deep pink flowers are borne at the end of long stems. Like pineapple sage, blackcurrant sage is hardy only to zone 8 though you might try protecting it from the occasional cold snap by wrapping it in a frost blanket. If the stems do die back, you will generally get a strong regrowth from the base of the plant in spring. It will grow happily in any kind of planter as well as directly in your garden soil; however, don't grow it in soil that is wet in the winter.

Opposite Pineapple sage forms a large, dense bush of tender shoots, which need protection in the winter. The leaves and stems are tinged with red at the edges.

Above This unusual variety of blackcurrant sage, with pretty pink and white flowers, is called 'Hot Lips'.

Useful Addresses

Societies

The Herb Society of America
9019 Kirtland Chardon Road.
Kirtland
OH 44094
Tel: 440 256 0514 (Office)
Fax: 440 256 0541
Monday–Thursday 9am–5pm
www.herbsociety.org
The society promotes the
knowledge, use, and delight
of herbs through educational
programs, research, and sharing
the experience of its members
with the community.

American Community Gardening Association
1777 East Broad Street
Columbus
OH 43203
Tel: 1 877 ASK ACGA (toll-free)
or 1 877 275 2242
Fax: 614 645 5921
info@communitygarden.org
www.communitygarden.org
The aim of the association is to
build community by increasing
and enhancing community
gardening and greening across
the United States and Canada.

Author's favorite gardening blogs

www.guardian.co.uk/lifeandstyle/
   allotment
www.bbc.co.uk/gardening
www.mytinyplot.co.uk
www.seedambassadors.org

Seed and plant suppliers

W. Atlee Burpee & Co.
300 Park Avenue
Warminster
PA 18974
Tel: 1 800 333 5808
www.burpee.com
Mail-order supplier of herb seeds.

Botanical Interests
660 Compton Street
Broomfield
Colorado 80020
Tel: 720 880 7293
www.botanicalinterests.com
Mail order supplier of organic herb
seeds.

Companion Plants
7247 N. Coolville Ridge Road
Athens
OH 45701
Tel: 740 592 4643
www.companionplants.com
Nursery supplying over 600
varieties of common and exotic
herb plants and seeds.

The Cook's Garden
PO Box C5030
Warminster
PA 18974
Tel: 1 800 457 9703
www.cooksgarden.com
Supplier of herb seeds and plants.

Debaggio's Herb Farm and Nursery
43494 Mountain View Drive
Chantilly
VA 20152
Tel: 703 327 6976
Herb growers.

Goodwin Creek Gardens
P.O. Box 83
Williams
OR 97544
Tel: 800 846 7359
www.goodwincreekgardens.com
Nursery supplying medicinal and
culinary herbs.

Park Seed Company
1 Parkton Avenue
Greenwood
SC 29647
Tel: 800 213 0076
www.parkseed.com
Supplier of herb seeds.

Peaceful Valley
P.O. Box 2209
125 Clydesdale Court
Grass Valley
CA 95945
Tel: 530 272 4769
www.groworganic.com
Supplier of organic plants and
seeds.

Seeds from Italy
P.O. Box 149
Winchester
MA 01890
Tel: 781 721 5904
www.growitalian.com
Mail order supplier of Italian herb
seeds.

Seeds of Change
Tel: 1 888 762 4240 (toll-free)
www.seedsofchange.com
Mail order supplier of organic
herb seeds.

Stokes Seeds
PO Box 548
Buffalo
New York 14240-0548
Tel: 716 695 6980
www.stokeseeds.com
Supplier of herb seeds.

The Thyme Garden Herb Company
20546 Alsea Highway
Alsea
Oregon 97324
Tel: 541 487 8671
www.thymegarden.com
Supplier of organically grown herb
plants and herb seeds.

Index

Author's acknowledgments:

Thanks to all my friends, gardeners, herb growers, and community gardeners, who shared their gardening knowledge and who allowed us to photograph in their plots, gardens, balconies, and terraces. In particular, thanks to Bill and Judy Hackett, Dan Morrell, Jill Patchett, and Mary White.

I am indebted, as always, to Heini Schneebeli for his work over the summer, taking the lovely photographs in this book.

Thanks also to Caroline Hughes for her thoughtful and sensitive photography.

I would like to thank Cindy Richards for commissioning me to write this book and therefore allowing me, in the process, to deepen my knowledge of herbs and herb growing.

I am grateful to Gillian Haslam for her experienced and friendly support, and to Eleanor van Zandt for her straightforward editing.